THE BRITISH ACADEMY

Lectures on

The Apocalypse

By

R. H. Charles, D.Litt., D.D.

Archdeacon of Westminster
Fellow of the British Academy

The Schweich Lectures

1919

WIPF & STOCK · Eugene, Oregon

Wipf and Stock Publishers
199 W 8th Ave, Suite 3
Eugene, OR 97401

The British Academy Lectures on The Apocolypse
The Schweich Lectures 1919
By Charles, R. H.
ISBN 13: 978-1-60608-242-3
Publication date 10/2/2008
Previously published by Oxford University Press, 1922

PREFACE

THESE Lectures were delivered in February, 1920, some months before the publication of my Commentary on the Apocalypse by Messrs. T. and T. Clark. Since the publication of this Commentary I have read all the reviews that have come under my notice—English, French, German, and Dutch. The greater number of these have pronounced favourably on most of the new departures, which I have taken alike in regard to the form of the Greek text, its Hebraistic character, its translation, and its interpretation. Practically all my reviewers have been brought to admit the necessity of an exhaustive knowledge of Jewish Apocalyptic, if we are to understand the Christian Apocalypse. This is something to be thankful for; since, as a rule, hitherto, even serious scholars, though possessed of the sorriest equipment in this department of knowledge, readily undertook to expound this great work.

As regards my reconstruction of the order of the text there has been less unanimity. But an examination of the objections that a small minority of my reviewers have advanced to my reconstruction and a renewed study on my own part of the subject as a whole during the last eighteen months have further confirmed me in the conclusion that most if not all of my reconstructions of the order of the text are wholly unaffected by their criticisms. To put the matter as courteously as possible, most of their objections have been due to a very incomplete knowledge alike of the manifold problems of the Apocalypse and of Apocalyptic.

But there is some excuse to be made on behalf of these critics. Their difficulties were aggravated by the fact that they had to criticize a very difficult work of nearly 1100 pages. It is not strange, therefore, that many of the arguments adduced by me in support of a new departure in textual or literary criticism, in interpretation, or the reconstruction of the order of the text, escaped their notice, seeing that the various converging lines of argument bearing on individual passages have not always been summarized, nor made accessible even in the index. Hence in some important questions this task has been left to the reader to do for himself. Now in the present Lectures, which can of course deal only with the main arguments and must perforce refer the reader for the details to my Commentary, I have summarized my new conclusions on the main problems of the Apocalypse, and in some cases the converging lines of evidence on which they are based. The serious student will observe that these conclusions are for the most part logically linked together, and that their evidence is cumulative.

I have mentioned only one of my critics by name, namely Dr. Burney, since his criticism, which accepts my theories of the Hebraistic character of the text, has helped me to correct an error in my translation of the text, though it is an error of which he is, strange to say, twice guilty in his own review. With this criticism I have dealt on pp. 32–4.

R. H. C.

4 LITTLE CLOISTERS,
   WESTMINSTER ABBEY.

CONTENTS

LECTURE I

Different methods of interpretation in the Early Churches arising from following problems: (a) Did the Apocalypse refer to the present and the future, or to the future alone? (b) Did it deal with concrete events, or was it a purely symbolical representation of the world's history? (c) Did it represent a succession of events following chronologically one upon another, or the same events under three successive series of Seven Seals, Seven Trumpets, and Seven Bowls? Study of Jewish Apocalypses and of the Apocalypse itself decides in favour of first of each of the three alternatives. Thus the Apocalypse deals with concrete events and is not a symbolical description of strife of good and evil; with concrete events of the author's own time and future events arising out of these (i.e. Contemporary-Historical Method), and with a strictly chronological succession of events (hence Recapitulation Method wrong).

Disabilities of earlier and of most modern interpreters—no knowledge of Jewish Apocalyptic—no exact knowledge of John's unique grammar, and their general acceptance of the spiritualizing method.[1]

Revival of study of Apocalypse by Joachim of Floris about 1200 A.D. Attack on the Papacy by Joachim and his followers in thirteenth and fourteenth centuries. Identification of the Papacy with the Antichrist. Reformation. Progress achieved, yet exegesis of Apocalypse continues to be unscientific.

Revival by Jesuits of Contemporary-Historical Method: adoption by the Reformers of two new methods—the Philological and the Literary-Critical. These three of permanent value. Literary-Critical method assumed three forms, two of which knowledge of John's grammar renders impossible. The third, i.e. the Fragmentary-Hypothesis, furnishes the element of permanent value in Literary-Critical method. This hypothesis assumes that the Apocalypse is from one author, but that the author has laid various sources under contribution. For the exact delimitation of these sources two things needed—a keen critical sense for dealing with the thought and contents of the Book, and an exact knowledge of its form, i.e. its style and grammar. Chief representatives of this method, such as Weizsäcker, Sabatier, Wellhausen and Bousset, possessed the former, but none of them, save Bousset, and he only in a secondary degree, possessed any knowledge of the latter.

---

[1] To these should be added their failure to recognize the frequent Hebraisms in the text (pp. 30–38), without a knowledge of which it is impossible to translate the text aright.

Much has been achieved of permanent value, but many problems have been left unsolved. The chief of these is connected with chaps. xx–xxii. Text of these chapters incoherent and self-contradictory. Unchastity, murder, and idolatry exist on the new earth after the final judgement. Conversion of the heathen still in progress. Bousset and others explain this by our author's incorporation of sources. This hypothesis breaks down in face of the strict unity of structure and orderly development of thought in i–xix, and of the linguistic unity of xx–xxii. Hence necessity for a hypothesis, which, while admitting Johannine authorship of these chapters, can explain the inherent contradictions. This is that John died before he had put the materials of these chapters in order, and that this was done by a disciple who failed wholly to understand his master's thought. pp. 9–12

Evidence for this hypothesis. Original order of xx–xxii. Descent of the first Jerusalem from heaven to be seat of Christ's kingdom for 1,000 years on earth. Description of this city. Expected in the Old Testament and Apocrypha. Surviving nations make pilgrimages to it as was expected in Judaism. No sorcerer to enter within its gates. Reign of the saints. Hence the original order was xx. 1–3, xxi. 9–xxii. 2, 14–15, 17, xx. 4–6. Next follow the attack of Gog and Magog on the Beloved City. Former heaven and earth vanish. Final Judgement—xx. 7–15. pp. 12–19

Creation of new heaven and earth and New Jerusalem—the eternal abode of the blessed, xxi. 5^a 4^d 5^b, 1–4^{abc}, xxii. 3–5. pp. 19–21

Epilogue. Hurtful activities of John's disciple or editor in xx–xxii. p. 21

LECTURE II

Hurtful activities of John's editor in i–xix. Some of the passages interpolated by him. i. 8 to be rejected on three grounds. pp. 22–23

viii. 7–12—an intrusion which exhibits an un-Semitic order of words: gives birth to the Recapitulation theory—a stultifying method: has made it impossible hitherto to discover the true significance of the Sealing in vii. 4–7: and the true interpretation of the phrase 'silence in heaven' in viii. 1. Original form of chapter viii. pp. 23–27

xiv. 3–4—an interpolation of the editor by means of which he excludes from the 144,000 that follow the Lamb, all women and all men except those that were strictly celibates—a pagan conception. Editor misunderstands ἀπαρχή. pp. 27–28

xiv. 15–17—the most stupid of the editor's interpolations, whereby he makes the Son of Man subordinate to an unnamed angel. xxii. 18^b–19—his last interpolation. pp. 28–29

The scholar who would master John's style and fit himself for the task of translating the Apocalypse must acquire a knowledge of its Hebraisms, its Greek Solecisms, and its poetical form. (1) The Hebraisms have been ignored by nearly every writer on the Apocalypse, and those who have recognized this element have done so in barely half a dozen passages. These Hebraisms have not been recognized by Bousset, Hort, Weiss, Moffatt, Swete, &c. Yet no translation can be a satisfactory rendering of the Apocalypse which fails to recognize or translate them accurately. Some examples of these Hebraisms and their mistranslations are i. 5–6, 18, ii. 23, xiv. 2–3, xv. 2–3, xii. 7. The Hebraism in i. 5–6 mistranslated in nearly every version till the present day. Hebrew writers after employing the participle often use finite verbs in subsequent parallel clauses. i. 18 wrongly translated hitherto.   pp. 29–32

A new departure in Hebrew syntax.   pp. 32–35 note

ii. 23—mistranslated and consequently misinterpreted. pp. 33–36

xiv. 2–3, xv. 2–3 mistranslated.   p. 36

xii. 7, xiii. 10—a hopeless crux of Greek grammarians. pp. 36–38

Where Hebrew and Greek words agree as to primary meanings, secondary meanings of the Hebrew wrongly assigned by our author to the Greek.   p. 38

(2) A critical knowledge of the Greek Solecisms in the Apocalypse indispensable to a mastery of John's style. These pervade every chapter that comes from his pen. But John's editor, being a better Grecian than his master, corrected some that he found intolerable in xx–xxii, and in some passages in the earlier chapters where he recast the text. Solecistic constructions following upon various cases of the participle καθήμενος.   pp. 38–39

Other solecisms: the solecism τῷ ἀγγέλῳ τῷ ἐν Ἐφέσῳ ἐκκλησίας.
                                                   pp. 39–40

(3) Poetical form. Of the twenty-two chapters only four are completely prose. John's book is a book of Songs. To print them as prose is to rob them of half their power. But it often does more. It deprives us of a critical means of detecting interpolations. This fact is valuable as a cause of criticism in xxi–xxii. The poetic form furnishes almost demonstrative evidence of the immediate sequence of xxii. 3–5 on xxi. 4^{abc}. The poem xxi. 5^a 4^d 5^b, 1–4^{abc}, xxii. 3–5.   pp. 41–42

If the following passages are written as verse, as they were intended to be, the parallelism helps us to recognize alien elements where these exist, and thus reinforces independently linguistic and contextual grounds for the rejection of such elements. Compare ii. 22–23, 26–28: xiv. 2^d 3^{abcd} 4^{cd} 5: xix. 11–13: xx. 4–6: vii. 9–10, 13–17: xviii. 11–13, 15–16, 14, 22–24.   pp. 42 48

xix. 1–4: xvi. 5^{bc}–7: xix. 5–9, consisting of three strophes of eight lines each.   pp. 48–49

Reasons for restoring xvi. 5^b–7 to its original context after xix. 4, and xiv. 12–13 after xiii. 18.   pp. 49–51

LECTURE III

LECTURE I

FROM the earliest ages of the Church it has been universally admitted that the Apocalypse is the most difficult book of the entire Bible. School after school has essayed its interpretation, and school after school has in turn retired in failure from the task. To only a few of these schools of interpretation can we make a passing allusion. From the second to the fourth centuries of the Christian era scholars were divided on the following questions. First: Did the Apocalypse refer to the present and the future, or only to the distant future? Secondly: Did it deal with definite concrete events, or was it to be regarded as a purely symbolical representation of the world's history? Thirdly: Did it represent a succession of events following chronologically one upon another, or the same events under three successive series of the Seven Seals, Seven Trumpets, and Seven Bowls? *Three main schools of interpretation in the Early Church.*

On all three questions most early expositors decided on the whole in the wrong. That this verdict is true we are forced to conclude, if we study Jewish Apocalyptic, beginning with Daniel and other early apocalypses down to the close of the first century of the Christian era. Such a study makes it clear that Jewish apocalypses are to be taken as referring first and chiefly to the times in which they were actually written;[1] and in the next place that they are not to be interpreted solely by symbolical and spiritual methods but as dealing with concrete issues and concrete events; that is, such apocalypses dealt with historical events and in the first instance with events contemporaneous with the age of their writers. Hence the Contemporary-Historical method is indispensable in the exegesis of all Jewish apocalypses. And what is true of such Jewish apocalypses is true also of the N. T. Apocalypse. It refers originally and essentially to events at the close of the first century of the Christian era, *Failure of the early expositors owing in part to their ignorance of Jewish Apocalyptic.* *The Contemporary-Historical method indispensable.*

---

[1] Jewish apocalypses have always been pseudonymous. Hence the actual time of their composition is here emphasized, not the alleged time.

B

though, of course, the truths it embodies are valid for all time. 'No great prophecy receives its full and final fulfilment in any single event or series of events. In fact, it may not be fulfilled at all in regard to the object against which it was primarily delivered by the prophet or seer. But, if it is the expression of a great moral or spiritual truth, it will of a surety be fulfilled at sundry times and in divers manners and in varying degrees of completeness in the history of the world.'[1]

The Apocalypse— not a mere allegory or symbolic representation of conflict of right and wrong. Secondly, it is no mere allegory or symbolical representation of the conflict of right and wrong. Hence we must—to give a single example, of false exegesis—exclude from the field of possible interpretation the view of Tyconius, the Donatist, that the Millennium is the period between the first and second advents of Christ. This view, which identified the Millennium with the entire period of the Church's history, was adopted by St. Augustine, and is still held by the Roman Church, and that in spite of the clear statement of the Apocalypse, that the Millennium or reign of the Saints cannot begin till the war of Armageddon is over—a war that is to be waged not only by physical arms but by spiritual, not only on land and sea but in the social, economic, and spiritual provinces of the individual, the national, and the international life.

Recapitulation theory must be rejected. And thirdly, like all Jewish apocalypses, which are not of composite authorship, the N. T. Apocalypse represents a succession of events following chronologically or logically one upon another, and not the same events under three successive series[2] of the Seven Seals, the Seven Trumpets, and the Seven

---

[1] See my *Commentary on Revelation*, vol. i, p. clxxxiii.

[2] The Book of Daniel, it is true, contains two distinct visions dealing with the same events in chapters ii and vii, but the former is a dream of ‘Nebuchadnezzar and is very brief and lacking in detail, whereas the latter is a vision of the Seer himself. Furthermore, Daniel is not a pure apocalypse, but partly an autobiography and partly an apocalypse. Thus the writer records events in Daniel's life extending from 605 to 544 B.C. Otherwise the chronological succession of events is in the main observed. Isa. xxiv–xxvii also on the whole observes a chronological order. See Gray, *Isaiah*, vol. i, pp. 397 sqq. 1 Enoch lxxiii–xc is strictly chronological and also the Assumption of Moses, and the Messiah Apocalypse in 2 Baruch liii–lxxiv. In the New Testament the Pauline Apocalypse in 1 Cor. xv. 22–8 is of the same character, and Little Apocalypse which has been worked into Mark xiii (and parallels in Matthew

Bowls. Thus the Recapitulation theory of Victorinus,[1] which in manifold forms and degrees has maintained itself from the third century to the present, must be unhesitatingly rejected.

It is true that some elements of sound methods of interpretation have been preserved in early writers of the Church such as Justin Martyr, Irenaeus, and Hippolytus, but the verdict on the interpretation of the third and fourth centuries as a whole cannot be other than adverse. But, when we consider the conditions under which scholars addressed themselves in those days to the study of the Apocalypse, we cannot but acknowledge that a valid interpretation was wholly beyond their reach. For such an interpretation they were without the necessary equipment. They had no knowledge at all, or at best the very slightest, of Jewish Apocalyptic—a disability under which ninety-nine out of every hundred expositors of the Apocalypse have laboured in the past. Next they had no knowledge of the unique grammar and style of their author—a disability by which more than ninety-nine out of a hundred expositors of our author are disqualified for such a task down to the present decade. And finally, their spiritualizing method, which enabled them to explain away every textual or other difficulty, closed their eyes to the real problems of the Apocalypse and to the impossible order in which the traditional text is preserved. *Some elements of sound interpretation are found in the early writers, but a valid interpretation of the Apocalypse was not possible for them owing to three disabilities. Their ignorance of Jewish Apocalyptic, of John's unique grammar and style, and their acceptance of the spiritualizing method.*

As I have dealt with the history of the interpretation of our author in my *Studies in the Apocalypse*, I will only advert to such methods as marked new epochs and generally epochs of advance in interpretation. During the Middle Ages no progress was made towards a saner interpretation till the time of Joachim of Floris, though the Book was studied and applied in every direction. This remarkable man found in the Apocalypse a complete history of the world. Though *A new age of interpretation begins with Joachim of Floris.*

and Luke): i. e. xiii. 7–8 (the travail pains of the Messiah or his initial distress); 14–20 (the actual tribulation); 24–7 (the Parousia). The same order is observed in the late Hebrew *Apocalypse of Elias* (ed. Buttenwieser, 1897). And so in numerous others. Now in the Apocalypse the Seals, Trumpets, and Bowls represent events in chronological order from chapter vi to xix. The Recapitulation theory, which assumes that these three orders of plagues deal with the same series of events, owes its origin to the interpolation of viii. 7–12 by John's editor (see later, p. 23 sqq.) and the misinterpretation of xiii. 15 and numerous other passages referring to the great tribulation or the universal martyrdom of the faithful. See p. 57 sqq.

[1] See my *Studies in the Apocalypse*, pp. 10–11.

His Francis-
can disciples
identify the
Pope with
the Anti-
christ.

loyal to the Church of Rome and regarding the Papacy as belonging to the eternal order of the Church, he, like Dante, freely criticized its appalling corruptions and its secularized character. This critical attitude to the Papacy was emphasized to an extreme degree by the fanatical section of the Franciscans, who came to regard Joachim as a prophet. These Franciscans made no distinction between the ideal of the Papacy and its realization in history. Thus soon after Joachim's day we find Peter John Olivi declaring the Papacy to be the mystical Antichrist and Ubertino di Casale identifying Boniface VIII with the first Beast in chapter xiii and Benedict XI with the second. This writer confirms the latter identification by showing that according to the value of the Greek letters $\beta\epsilon\nu\epsilon\delta\iota\kappa\tau os = 666$, the number of the Antichrist ($\beta = 2$, $\epsilon = 5$, $\nu = 50$, $\epsilon = 5$, $\delta = 4$, $\iota = 10$, $\kappa = 20$, $\tau = 300$, $o = 70$, $\sigma = 200$).[1] Thus the writers of the thirteenth and fourteenth centuries forged the weapons which the Reformers of the sixteenth used against Rome.

Only the student of these centuries can recognize how opportune was the appearance of this school of apocalyptic founded by Joachim and his followers.[2]

The appear-
ance of this
school coin-
cides with
the period
when the
Papacy
reached its
zenith under
Innocent III.

The Papacy had just reached the zenith of its power under Innocent III. It claimed supreme authority alike over things sacred and secular. In his inaugural sermon in 1198 Innocent declared: 'I am the Vicar of Jesus Christ, the successor of Peter; I am placed between God and man, less than God, greater than man: I judge all men but can be judged of none.' The establishment of the Inquisition a few years later followed logically on such claims: likewise the massacre of the Albigenses, and the demand that the civil authorities should henceforth exterminate all who refused to accept the dogmas laid down by the Church.

Hence the attack of this school of apocalyptic on Rome emboldened kings and statesmen to resist the temporal encroachments of the Papacy, and nerved alike men of thought

---

[1] I have found this identification also on the margin of a Greek manuscript of the Apocalypse (thirteenth century) but in another and later hand, though four other alternatives are given: $\tau\epsilon\iota\tau\hat{a}\nu$, $\pi\epsilon\rho\sigma a\hat{\iota}os$, $\lambda a\tau\epsilon\hat{\iota}\nu os$, $\epsilon\hat{v}a\nu\theta\acute{a}s$. The manuscript is no. 468 in the National Library of Paris. Benedict XI was pope from 1303 to 1304. He was beatified but not canonized in 1733.

[2] See my *Studies in the Apocalypse*, pp. 21 sqq.

and men of deep spiritual experience to resist its intellectual and religious encroachments : while monks, scholars, artisans, and the masses generally gathered from its teaching in the thirteenth and fourteenth centuries the strength needful to withstand oppression, whether emanating from Church or State.   Down to the close of the twelfth century the Church had satisfied the religious and intellectual needs of men : it had inspired the race with new and lofty ideals, and had rendered incalculable services in every department of social, industrial, and national life.   But henceforth the Papacy became the foe of progress, and those who sought for further light on questions religious, metaphysical or scientific, had to look elsewhere than to mediaeval Catholicism.   Moreover, in the course of the fourteenth and fifteenth centuries the corruption of the Church advanced by leaps and bounds, and the enthronement of Alexander VI on the seat of St. Peter, not to speak of others hardly less infamous, gave no little justification to the writings of Joachim's school, which had identified Rome with the Scarlet Woman and the Pope with the Antichrist.

The Church led the way in religious, intellectual, and social matters till the twelfth century. Thenceforward it became almost without exception a reactionary force.

Such a period of corruption and ferment, social and ecclesiastical, was threatening the civilized world with the return of civil and religious anarchy, when the Reformation emerged and secured to a considerable degree liberty of conscience for religious men and liberty of thought for thinkers and men of science.

The opposition to the reactionary Church comes to a head in the Reformation.

But we must press on.   Though the Reformation conferred innumerable benefits on the world, its exegesis of the Apocalypse was for many decades just as uncritical and worthless as that of the scholars of the Roman Church.   While the Reformers identified Papal Rome with the Antichrist, the Papal scholars retorted by condemning their assailants as the collective Antichrist.   Both alike were hopelessly unscientific.   Neither the papalists nor the antipapalists had any sound method to guide them.   Both alike regarded the Apocalypse as a *prophetic compendium or handbook—not merely of Church history but of the world's history.*   Hence their efforts were spent in the hopeless task of interpreting the symbolic language of the Apocalypse in such a way as to read into it the history of all things sacred and secular.   Since they had no scientific method to guide them—and were thus at liberty to attach almost any meaning to any symbol and to explain away any statement

But the exegesis of the Apocalypse continues to be unscientific alike among the Reformers and their Papal opponents.

that conflicted with their theories, they generally succeeded in gaining the authentication of the Apocalypse for their own particular systems of Church and State.

But anarchy and unreason cannot maintain themselves indefinitely. At length from the welter of the conflicting schools of exegesis three methods emerged, which are indispensable for the interpretation of the Apocalypse. One of these was the revival of the Contemporary-Historical method by the Jesuists Alcasar, Ribeira, and others. This method, as we have already recognized, implies that the author of the Apocalypse addressed himself first and chiefly to the events of his own time. This method has under various guises rightly achieved a permanent place in all scientific interpretation of the Apocalypse. The second is a very modest form of the Philological method, which we owe to the Reformers Camerarius, Beza, Castellio, and others. The school, which adopted this method and devoted itself exclusively to the philological study of the Apocalypse, owed its birth in no small degree to the feeling of despair that had arisen amongst the best scholars of the sixteenth century of ever discovering the mysteries of the Seven-sealed Book. The hopelessness of arriving at trustworthy and permanent results by the methods of interpretation current in that century appear to have withheld Calvin from writing a Commentary on the Apocalypse. And yet Calvin was by far the greatest exegete of that age. His discretion in declining this task drew forth from his contemporary, the younger Scaliger, who ranks amongst the foremost classical scholars of all time, the remark, 'Calvinus sapit quod in Apocalypsin non scripsit', 'Calvin shows his prudence in that he has not written a commentary on the Apocalypse'.

In the interpretation of the Apocalypse many a great reputation has found its grave—at least so far as it has committed itself to adventures in this department of study. Of well-known scholars who have added no lustre to their names in this field we might mention Whiston, Sir Isaac Newton, Dupuis, Morosow, Hommel, and others. The cause of such gigantic failures is to be traced to their profound ignorance alike of the language of the N.T. Apocalypse, and of the nature and contents of apocalyptic in general. Hence the philological study of the Apocalypse was a move in the right direction. Its aim was to displace idle speculation in

Margin notes:

i. Contemporary-Historical method revived by the Jesuits.

ii. The Philological method founded by the Reformers.

the province of what rightly or wrongly it regarded as un-
knowable by an exact knowledge of what, it held, could be
known. Unhappily this movement did not develop as it
should have done into the propaedeutic necessary for all
serious students of the Apocalypse—a propaedeutic involving
an accurate knowledge of its grammar and of apocalyptic
in general.

The third method—the Literary-Critical—owes its origin
to Grotius, the great Dutch scholar, jurist and statesman.
Grotius was the first Protestant scholar to break definitely
with the antipapal interpretation of the Apocalypse, and to
lead the Reformed Churches to the recognition and use of the
Contemporary-Historical method. Herein he was no more
original than the Jesuists whose guidance he had followed.
But Grotius went further. He recognized that different
sections of the Apocalypse presupposed different historical
relations and dates, and found therein the explanation of the
fact that the early writers of the Church were divided, and
rightly divided, amongst themselves as to the date of the
Apocalypse itself. Hence he conjectured that the Apocalypse
was composed of several visions which were committed to
writing at different times and in different places before and
after the destruction of Jerusalem. Grotius was thus the
founder of the Literary-Critical method.

Grotius died in 1645. Yet it was not till the closing decades
of the nineteenth century that his suggestions bore fruit,
consciously or unconsciously, in the three developments of
this method that appealed to the suffrages of the learned
world. These were the Redactional-Hypothesis, the Sources-
Hypothesis, the Fragmentary-Hypothesis.

The Redactional-Hypothesis presupposes a plurality of
editors. According to this theory the original autograph was
edited or enlarged by a succession of editors, till it attained
the form in which it has come down to us. The Sources-
Hypothesis presupposes a plurality of independent sources,
whether two, three, four, or more, which were subsequently
put together by one or more editors. Amongst the advocates
of the first method are Völter, Vischer, Harnack, Kohler,
Johannes Weiss, and Von Soden, and amongst advocates of
the second are Spitta, Schmidt, and Briggs.[1]

iii. Literary-
Critical
method
founded by
Grotius.

Rise of three
new hypo-
theses.
i. Redactional-
Hypothesis.
ii. Sources-
Hypothesis.

---

[1] These two methods are not mutually exclusive, as a study of the
various hypotheses amply shows.

While these two methods have made undoubted contribu-
tions towards the solution of certain difficulties in the Apocalypse, they must be frankly rejected as a whole, seeing that
the vocabulary, grammar, and style of the Apocalypse in the
main are unique over against all other Greek literature, and,
as such, they make such hypotheses thereby arbitrary and
absolutely impossible.

The third hypothesis maintains the relative unity of the
book but assumes that its author in certain sections made use
of other materials. This method has been advocated by
Weizsäcker, Bousset, and Wellhausen in Germany, Sabatier
in France, Porter in the U.S., and Anderson Scott and Moffat
in England. The last three scholars are conservative in their
criticism and to a great extent are disciples of Bousset.

This hypothesis is in my opinion the one that must in some
form be adopted by all serious scholars. It recognizes, as
Grotius had already done, that certain sections of the
Apocalypse were written at different dates, but it goes further,
and proves that certain sections of it are not from our author's
own hand but were adopted by him and recast more or less
with a view to the setting forth of his great theme.

This hypothesis is most satisfactory as a general explanation
of the facts, but many difficulties arise when it is put into
actual practice, especially by those who have not studied
the grammar and style of the Apocalypse. In such a case the
personal equation enters disastrously, and especially in the
criticism of Wellhausen, the greatest of the scholars just
mentioned. This splendid and original scholar, whose name
is connected inseparably with O. T. criticism, has, it must be
confessed, failed lamentably in his criticism of the Apocalypse.

Even an elementary knowledge of the unique character of
John's grammar would have saved him from the numerous
pitfalls into which he has fallen.[1] And yet Wellhausen's

---

[1] To give a couple of instances. In his *Analyse der Offenbarung
Johannis* (p. 4) he assigns i. 1-3, xxii. 18-19 to the final editor of the
Apocalypse. But he ought to have recognized that in i. 3 we have
the first of the *seven* beatitudes. It is no accident that there are *seven*
beatitudes, no more and no less. Hence i. 1-3 must come from the
writer who is answerable for the whole seven. Next he assigns the
Letters to the seven Churches to an earlier writer than the Seer. A
knowledge of the unique idioms of chapters ii–iii would have saved him
from this blunder.

treatise is full of suggestive remarks, which, whether right
or wrong, cannot fail to lead to a more thorough study of
the text.

Bousset's *Commentary on the Apocalypse*, which is un-
questionably the ablest that has yet been published, exhibits
a larger knowledge of John's grammar than any of his
predecessors or his successors. But it was not exhaustive
enough to save him on the one hand from acknowledging as
John's work passages that he ought to have excised, or, on the
other hand, from branding as alien sources passages that
belong to the essence of the Apocalypse and have undoubtedly
come from John's hand.

I have now shortly reviewed the work of my predecessors
in this field, and, while I have criticized their failures, I have
at the same time been careful to emphasize their real contri-
butions to the interpretation of our author. As regards my
own work I gratefully and gladly acknowledge my indebtedness to every real scholar who has worked over this field.
Even where I have had most occasion to pass censure, I have
often learnt most, as in the case of such scholars as Völter,
Spitta, Johannes Weiss, and Wellhausen. *The present writer's indebtedness to every real scholar in this field.*

Most writers on the Apocalypse have failed not only to
interpret it but even to recognize its real difficulties. In fact,
it is only scholars who have in some degree made a subject
their own that are in a position to recognize its difficulties.
To recognize the difficulties or problems of a subject is the
first step towards their solution. Hence, if we wish to qualify
ourselves for this task in connexion with the Apocalypse, we
must first master Jewish Apocalyptic, and next the unique
grammar and style of the Apocalypse. *The first step towards the interpretation of the Apocalypse is to qualify oneself to recognize its problems.*

It is now my task to show the new steps that exegesis must
take if it is to unravel many of the outstanding problems
of the Apocalypse. I will begin with the last three chapters,
since it was in connexion with these that I discovered the
solution of one of the main difficulties of the book—a solution
which has led to many discoveries in the earlier chapters. As
far back as the year 1893, in a publication issued by the
Oxford University Press,[1] I drew attention to the fact that
in chap. xxi. 1-2, though the former heaven and the former
earth had passed away and their place been taken by a new
heaven and a new earth and by a New Jerusalem that *First step to be taken towards the solution of these problems.* *Irreconcilable statements in xx-xxii.*

---

[1] *The Book of Enoch*, 1893, p. 45.

descended on the new earth, yet in chap. xxii. 11 all classes of sinners and evildoers are described as still living outside the gates of the New Jerusalem on the new earth. But, since the New Jerusalem does not come down from heaven till Satan is cast into the lake of fire, till the final judgement is past, and sin and death are at an end for ever, and a new and glorious heaven and earth have been created to take the place

Unchastity, murder, idolatry, exist on the new earth!

of the old, it is not possible for sorcerers, unchaste persons, murderers, and idolaters to exist anywhere in this new world. A greater contradiction in thought and language is hardly conceivable. Again, since the new earth is inhabited only by the righteous and blessed, on whom the second death could have no effect, and God himself dwells amongst them, the statement that the leaves of the tree of life are for the healing

After the final judge-ment the conversion of the nations still in progress in the heavenly Jerusalem! Explanation of this anomaly.

of the nations is unintelligible; for this implies that evil and sin still prevail and that the evangelization of the nations is still in progress. On the other hand, such a statement would be full of force and meaning if it was made in reference to the period of the Millennial Kingdom. For during the reign of Christ for 1,000 years, the world will be evangelized afresh, as we are told three times in the earlier chapters, xi. 15, xiv. 6–7, xv. 4. Hence, if these statements come from John's hand they can only apply to the further period of grace accorded to the nations during these 1,000 years, and that the nations take advantage of this period of grace we learn

Millennial Kingdom still in existence.

from xxi. 24–7; for only on the supposition that the Millennial Kingdom is still in existence can we explain this passage:

'And the nations shall walk in the light thereof,
And the kings of the earth shall bring their glory into it,
And the gates thereof shall not be shut day or *night*.[1]
And they shall bring the glory and honour of the nations
    into it:
And there shall not enter into it anything unclean or he
    that maketh an abomination or a lie;
But only they that are written in the Lamb's book of life.'

These con-tradictions postulate one or other of two con-clusions.

Now from the above contradictions—and these are but a few of them—it follows either (a) that a considerable part

---

[1] The text reads 'for there shall be no night there'—a corruption due in part to xxii. 5 where the New Jerusalem, the everlasting abode of the blessed, is described. But here the heavenly Jerusalem is only the temporary seat of the Messiah's kingdom. See my *Commentary*, vol. ii, p. 173.

of xx–xxii is not from the hand of our author, or (b) that, if it is from his hand, it is disarranged.

The first solution (a) is that adopted by most of the leading scholars of the past thirty years. Thus, while Erbes and Bousset trace these chapters to two sources, Völter, Weyland, Johannes Weiss, and Wellhausen assume three, Spitta finds himself obliged to postulate four. Formerly I adopted Bousset's solution of the problem, but in due course was obliged to abandon it owing to two insuperable difficulties. (a) The first of these is that the more closely we study the first nineteen chapters, the more strongly convinced we become of the structural unity of these chapters, and the clear and orderly development of thought, working up steadily to a climax—facts which do not exclude the occasional use and adaptation of sources. This being so, how is it that the last three chapters show no such orderly development, but rather a chaos of conflicting conceptions? (β) But the second difficulty is still greater. The hypothesis that the conflicting conceptions in these three chapters is due to the incorporation of one or more sources breaks down hopelessly in the face of their linguistic unity. With the exception of about three verses these three chapters are from the hand to which we owe the bulk of the preceding chapters. To this conclusion I was led by an exhaustive study of the vocabulary, idioms, and style of the Apocalypse. The assumption of a plurality of authors for these chapters is thus rendered impossible. The results of this study of the idioms and syntax of our author I have embodied in a Short Grammar of the Apocalypse which is published in the Introduction to my *Commentary*.[1] The knowledge so acquired provides the chief criterion for determining the authorship of many different sections of the Apocalypse.

Thus, whilst in the last three chapters it compels us to acknowledge the hand of John throughout, in earlier chapters it just as strongly obliges us to brand as interpolations certain passages which every student of the Apocalypse has hitherto accepted, and which at the same time have perverted or made unintelligible the original meaning of the context into which they have been forcibly thrust. Here it is that the philological method comes into its own.

But to return. Since these chapters are from the hand of

Marginal notes:

(a) Either the text is interpolated.

This hypothesis untenable; (a) since i–xix shows a strict unity of structure, and an orderly development of thought, xx–xxii cannot be chaotic and self-contradictory.

(β) xx–xxii saving three verses is from John's hand, as their grammar and style prove,

just as they brand certain passages in i–xix as interpolations.

Hence since xx–xxii are

---

[1] See my *Commentary*, vol. i, pp. cxvii–clix.

chaotic and self-contradictory and yet from John's hand, the present order of the text is not the original order.

John, and since the order of thought in these chapters is confused and chaotic, it follows that the text does not stand in the orderly sequence originally designed by the author, seeing that the orderly and dramatic development of thought are characteristic of our author.

To what cause, we must now ask, is this almost incredible disorder due? Since no accidental transposition of the text of these three chapters could explain its frequent and intolerable confusions, the only hypothesis adequate to account for them appears to be that John died when he had completed i–xx. 3 of his work, and that the materials for its completion, which were ready in a series of visions from John's own hand, were put together by an unintelligent disciple in what seemed to him to be the most probable order.

Only hypothesis adequate to explain the above phenomena.

Since in my *Commentary* I have given at length adequate proofs for this conclusion, I will not repeat them here.

We must now attempt to reconstruct the text in its original order.

Having now recognized the manifest disorder of the traditional text, the next duty awaiting us is to recover the original order and so to reconstruct the text as John designed it. In the main this is not difficult to the student who has mastered the earlier chapters and our author's style, and is also familiar with Jewish Apocalyptic.

Let us now show briefly how we may recover the original order in which these chapters were written.

xx. 1–3 stood rightly at the beginning. Satan imprisoned for 1,000 years during the Millennial Kingdom.

The first three verses of the twentieth chapter recount the casting down of Satan into the abyss and his imprisonment therein for 1,000 years. The traditional text next gives a vision of Christ's Kingdom on earth for 1,000 years, but makes no reference to the seat of this kingdom and yet such a reference cannot be wanting. Was the historical Jerusalem intended as such? This is impossible for two reasons. In the first place it was in ruins. In the next the attitude of the Seer was so hostile to it, that, even if it had not been in ruins, he could not have regarded it as the seat of Christ's Kingdom. As far back as chap. xi. 8 the Seer speaks of the historical Jerusalem as that 'great city which is spiritually called Sodom and Egypt, where our Lord was crucified'. The historical Jerusalem is thus excluded. If, then, our author gives any description of the new centre of Christ's Kingdom, where is it to be found? The answer is at once obvious, if we look further on. It is in chaps. xxi–xxii. Here we find the description of two different Jerusalems. One of them is called 'the holy

But what is the capital of this Kingdom? Not the historical city which is a spiritual Sodom and Egypt, even if it were not in ruins,

but the material Jerusalem

city, New [1] Jerusalem' (xxi. 2), the other 'the holy city Jerusalem' (xxi. 10). Both are said to come down from heaven, but the former is said to descend *from the new heaven on the new earth*, whereas the context of the second vision presupposes the descent of the second city *from the first heaven on the first earth*. These two cities are seen in two distinct visions. The vision of the New Jerusalem is seen from some point in space; for the Seer tells us that the first heaven and the first earth had already passed away (xxi. 1).

[margin: which descends from heaven on the present earth, xxi. 9–xxii. 2, and is absolutely distinct from the New Jerusalem which descends from the new heaven on the new earth, xxi. 1–2.]

With this fact he had acquainted us already in xx. 11, where we read:

'I saw a great white throne and him that sat upon it,
From whose face the earth and the heaven fled away,
And no place was found for them.'

A description of this New Jerusalem is given in the opening verses of xxi, but this description breaks off fragmentarily with xxi. 4, the last line of a four-line stanza being omitted. Happily, as we shall discover presently, this fourth line and the two final stanzas of the description are preserved in xxii. 2–5.

[margin: Description of the New Jerusalem.]

Let us now turn to the second [2] vision which deals with the second city, 'the holy city Jerusalem'. Now, we should observe that whereas the first vision (xxi. 1–5) presupposes

[margin: The holy city Jerusalem in the second[2] vision was a familiar]

---

[1] The newness in character, purity, and permanence of the New Kingdom is a favourite theme in the Apocalypse. It is not new in the sense of being a glorified repetition of the old world that then was, that is, it was not new as regards time (νέος) but new as regards quality (καινός). This character belongs not only to every part of the kingdom, but to all that dwell therein. Each of its citizens is to bear a new name (ὄνομα καινόν ii. 17, iii. 12). John would have agreed with Paul in calling such a man 'a new man' (καινὸν ἄνθρωπον Eph. iv. 24) or 'a new creature' (καινὴ κτίσις 2 Cor. v. 17, Gal. vi. 15). The Seer beholds in a vision, after the former heaven and earth had passed away, 'a new heaven and a new earth' (οὐρανὸν καινὸν καὶ γῆν καινήν xxi. 1), and 'a New Jerusalem' (Ἰερουσαλὴμ καινήν xxi. 2). After the old creation had passed away God declares, 'Behold I make all things new' (ἰδοὺ καινὰ ποιῶ πάντα xxi. 5ᵇ). Whatever is new, whether person or thing, in this sense belongs to the eternal world of being. See my *Commentary*, vol. i. 92, 146; vol. ii. 204.

[2] I call this the second vision in accordance with its place in the traditional text, but this vision, of course, should precede, and did precede the vision of the New Jerusalem in the Seer's original draft of his work.

expectation
in Jewish
Apocalyptic.

the destruction of the first heaven and the first earth (xx. 11,
xxi. 1), the second vision on the other hand (xxi. 9–xxii. 2,
14–15, 17) presupposes both as still existent. The Seer, who
in the first vision had seen from some point in space the
New Jerusalem descend from the new heaven on the new
earth, sees in the second vision from a high mountain on the
earth the holy city Jerusalem descend from heaven to the
earth on which the Seer is standing.[1]

In keeping with the fact just stated we recognize the
thoroughly material nature of this second city. It is, therefore, a city most suitable for the present earth. This city
was of pure gold. It had walls of jasper and gates of pearl,
and the foundations of its wall were of twelve different
precious stones. Now this conception of the Holy City during
the Messianic reign was one long familiar to the Jewish
nation. Thus in Is. liv. 11–12 the earthly Zion is described
as follows :

' Behold I will set thy bases in rubies,
    And thy foundations in sapphires.
    And I will make of jasper thy pinnacles,
    And thy gates of carbuncles, and all thy border of jewels.'

And in Tobit xiii. 16–18 :

' And the gates of Jerusalem shall be builded with sapphire
      and emerald,
    And all thy walls with precious stones.
    The towers of Jerusalem shall be builded with gold,
    And their battlements with pure gold.
    The streets of Jerusalem shall be paved
    With carbuncle and stones of Ophir,
    And the gates of Jerusalem shall utter hymns of gladness,
    And all her houses shall say : Hallelujah.'

The holy Jerusalem, therefore, in the second vision is essentially
that which was expected by the Jews on the present earth, as
the capital of the Messianic Kingdom.[2]

Description
of the Holy

The passages from Isaiah and Tobit guide us in the inter-

---

[1] For earlier and contemporary works, where the expectation of the
setting up of a new and holy Jerusalem on the present earth, see
1 En. xc. 29 ; T. Dan. v. 12 ; 4 Ezra vii. 26, x. 25 sqq.

[2] Cf. also Isa. lx. 10, 11, 13, 17 ; Haggai ii. 3, 4, 7–9 ; Zech. ii. 1–5 ;
1 Enoch xc. 29, where God Himself removes the old city and builds in its
stead a glorious city to stand for ever on the present earth : 2 Bar.
xxxii. 2. See also my *Commentary*, vol. ii. 158–61, 170 sq.

pretation of this city constructed of gold and precious stones City in xxi.
in the Apocalypse. These are not to be taken literally. They 9–xxii. 2 poetical
are poetical and suggestive: symbols of the spiritual glory that rather than
belongs to the chief seat of Christ's Kingdom. Every good and literal.
perfect gift cometh down from heaven. The City of God will
notwithstanding all hindrances be realized on earth. And yet
there are elements in the description that cannot be interpreted
symbolically.[1]

Thus we conclude that the city described in xxi. 9–xxii. Second
2, 14–15, 17 is the seat of Christ's Kingdom on earth. The expectation common to
very phrase that describes it, 'the holy city, Jerusalem' our author
(xxi. 10), is borrowed directly from Isa. lii. 1. and Jewish prophecy.

Another characteristic belonging to this city is likewise The surviving
found in Isaiah, other O. T. prophets, in Tobit, and in most of nations are to make
the Pseudepigrapha. This is that the nations [2] and the kings pilgrimages

---

[1] It seems impossible to interpret symbolically the return of the
martyrs to the earth. As I have shown in the third lecture, pp. 57–61,
the Seer expected a universal martyrdom of all the faithful. This
forecast of a universal martyrdom naturally led to recasting of the
traditional expectation of the Millennial Kingdom. If the world was to be
evangelized afresh, this evangelization could not be effected save through
supernatural intervention, seeing that all the faithful were to be martyred
before the advent of the Kingdom. See my *Commentary*, vol. ii. 456–7.

[2] These are the neutral nations that have not oppressed the Christian
Church. This idea is borrowed from Jewish Apocalyptic; cf. 2 Baruch
lxxii. 2–4: 'When ... the time of My Messiah is come, he shall summon
all the nations, and some of them he shall spare, and some of them
he shall slay. ... Every nation, which knows not Israel and has not
trodden down the seed of Jacob, shall indeed be spared. ... But all
those who have ruled over you or have known you, shall be given up to
the sword.' Pss. Sol. xvii. 27: 'He (the Messiah) shall destroy the godless
nations with the word of his mouth. ...' 32: 'And he shall have the
heathen nations to serve under his yoke.' In 1 Enoch lvi. 8, xc. 18 the
hostile nations are destroyed and the rest are converted to Judaism, xc. 30.
In 4 Ezra xiii. 37–8 the ungodly and hostile nations are to be destroyed
and endure torments in the next world, whereas other Gentiles are to be
pardoned, xiii. 13: cp. 1 Enoch x. 21, 22, xci. 14. Naturally the Romans
as the great oppressors were to be destroyed and live for ever in Tartarus,
Or. Sibyl. v. 174 sqq. Multitudes of other passages could be cited from
the Apocrypha, the Pseudepigrapha, and the Talmud in support of the
above facts (see Volz, *Jüdische Eschat.*, pp. 275, 322 sqq.), and yet one of
my reviewers, who has himself written a Commentary on the Apocalypse,
asserts that 'this distinction of the neutral and active foes' has
originated with myself. Here, as frequently, he and other Commentators
have failed to understand the Apocalypse through their ignorance of
Jewish Apocalyptic and of other no less vital departments of knowledge.

to the Holy
City and are
healed of
their
spiritual
diseases.
of the earth would make pilgrimages to Jerusalem and bring their wealth and their glory into it, and that its gates would not be closed day or night (xxi. 24–6). These very words are derived from Isaiah :

' Thy gates also shall be open continually ;
They shall not be shut day nor night ;
That the riches of the nations may be brought unto thee,
Their kings leading [1] the way ' (lx. 11).
' And nations shall come to thy light,
And kings to the brightness of thy rising ' (Is. lx. 3).

With the description of the holy city Jerusalem in Tobit xiii. 16–18, which we have quoted above, its author combines this same expectation (xiii. 10–11), as also does the author of the Psalms of Solomon (xvii. 34).

Third
expectation
common to
our author
and Jewish
prophecy—
no sinner
or unclean
person shall
enter its
gates.
A third characteristic that our book shares with Isaiah, Ezekiel, and later writers is that it teaches (xxi. 27) that though evil and unclean persons live without the city as naturally upon this present earth, none shall be allowed to enter the city :

' For henceforth there shall no more enter into thee
The uncircumcised and the unclean ' (Is. lii. 1).

The same expectation is set forth in the Psalms of Solomon (xvii. 29) :

' And he shall not suffer unrighteousness to lodge any more
in their midst,
Nor shall there dwell with them any man that knoweth
wickedness.'

Similarly in the Apocalypse the Seer tells us that outside the gates of the city there is every kind of evil.

Hence the nations that survived the judgements in chapter xix of the Apocalypse are represented in conformity with Jewish prophecy and Apocalyptic as going in pilgrimage to the Holy City—the seat of Christ's Kingdom—and of being healed therein of their spiritual and moral diseases, xxi. 24–6, xxii. 2. From this city are excluded all that are unclean or that make an abomination or a lie. Hence outside its gates are the sorcerers and the unchaste and the murderers and all other persistent offenders, xxi. 27, xxii. 15. Such statements, it may be added, are unintelligible save of a Holy City founded on this earth before the final judgement.

[1] An emendation accepted by most modern scholars.

'Without are the dogs and the sorcerers,
And the fornicators and the murderers, and the idolaters.
And every one that loveth and maketh a lie' (xxii. 15).
'And there shall not enter into it anything unclean or one
      that maketh an abomination or a lie :
But only they that are written in the Lamb's book of life'
                                          (xxi. 27).

This characteristic cannot belong to the New Jerusalem situated in the new heaven or on the new earth. It is only possible in connexion with the city founded on such an earth as ours; and under such conditions as we find in Isaiah and in the Psalms of Solomon, and later Jewish writings.[1]

We have now given sufficient evidence to prove that in xxi. 9–xxii. 2, 14–15, 17 we have a description of the Jerusalem that was to descend from heaven on the present earth and to form the Capital of Christ's Kingdom during the reign of 1,000 years. This vision, therefore, should be restored immediately after xx. 3. The evidence already furnished for the dislocation of xxi. 9–xxii. 2, 14–15, 17 from their right context after xx. 3, if not logically conclusive, practically amounts to a demonstration, especially if the text is submitted to a detailed examination, as I have done in my *Commentary*.

xxi. 9–xxii. 2, 14–15, 17 is therefore a description of the Jerusalem that was to be the seat of Christ's Kingdom on earth, and should be restored after xx. 3.

I have already shown that the description of the heavenly city—xxi. 9–xxii. 2, 14–15, 17—is of the same character as that recorded above in Isaiah or Tobit, and other Jewish works, and that these writers all agreed in this that the Holy City was to be founded on the present earth. I have also shown that the details of this heavenly city in the Apocalypse presuppose the present earth as its seat; that certain neutral nations still survive on the earth, not having been annihilated either by war, or by the Word of God in xix. 11–21, or in the Final Judgement in xx. 11–15, as the traditional order of the text presupposes, and that in accordance with the prophecies of the conversion of the Gentiles in xi. 15, xiv. 6–7, xv. 4 as well as in the Jewish prophets, these nations, headed by their kings as in Isaiah, make pilgrimages to the holy city, bring their glory and honour into it, receive spiritual healing within

---

[1] In the Hebrew Book of Elias (third century A. D.) Jerusalem descends from heaven to the present earth, built of precious stones and pearls, to be the habitation of the faithful Jews (see Buttenwieser, *Hebräische Elias-Apokalypse*, 1897, pp. 25, 67). Naturally, as in a Jewish work, the Temple is represented as standing in it.

its walls, and assimilate the divine truths that make them heirs to immortality, that is, to use the symbolical language of the Seer, eat of the tree of life. I have shown also that all the individual· members of these nations do not avail themselves of these privileges; for that outside its gates are sorcerers and whoremongers and idolaters and whosoever loveth and maketh a lie.

Since, therefore, all the features in the description of the heavenly city postulate a time anterior to the Final Judgement, we must transpose xxi. 9–xxii. 2, 14–15, 17 before the Final Judgement in xx. 11–15, and regard the Holy City as the seat of the Millennial Kingdom. Nay more, it is possible to restore it to its exact position in xx; for while on the one hand it must be placed after xx. 1–3 which recounts the chaining of Satan in the abyss, on the other it must be met before the vision of the glorified martyrs in xx. 4–6 who reign with Christ on earth for 1,000·years.

Restoration of xx. 9–xxii. 2, 14–15, 17 to its original context after xx. 3 and before xx. 4–6.

I may add here that 4 Ezra, which is a Jewish Apocalypse, *connects*, as does our restored text, *the advent of the Messiah and the heavenly Jerusalem with a temporary kingdom on the earth* (vii. 26–8).[1] This section of 4 Ezra may be earlier in date than the Apocalypse.

During the Millennial Kingdom the nations are to be evangelized afresh according to three passages in the earlier chapters. But in the traditional text there is no hint of this. Yet xxi. 24–7 imply this fresh evangelization.

We have now recovered the original order of the text so far: xx. 1–3, xxi. 9–xxii. 2, 14–15, 17, xx. 4–6. Obviously xx. 7–10 follows immediately, in which the attack of Gog and Magog on 'the Beloved City'[2] is described, and their destruction with the casting of Satan into the lake of fire. From this temporal judgement on Gog and Magog we naturally pass to the Final Judgement in xx. 11–15. Heaven and Earth

Immediately after the xxi. 9–xxii. 2, 14–15, 17 we should read xx. 4–6: then 7–10—the attack of the heathen on the 'Beloved City', and

---

[1] In 4 Ezra xiii. 32–6 we have the Messiah and Jerusalem coming down from heaven again associated. Box attributes xiii. 36 to the redactionist, but it is possibly original. If so, it should be restored immediately after xiii. 32. In the *Apocalypse of Elias* (Steindorff) this expectation is also found; also in the *Sepher Elias* (Buttenwieser), which is preserved only in Hebrew.

[2] 'The Beloved City' is the city which came down from heaven (xxi. 10). It cannot be the historical city Jerusalem, which is designated spiritually as 'Sodom and Egypt' in xi. 8.

pass away : only the great white throne is visible in illimitable space, and before that throne all the dead are judged, and death and hell are cast into the lake of fire.

So far we are on secure ground in our reconstruction of the text, and the next step to be taken in this reconstruction is no less certain; for here the manuscripts have to a considerable degree preserved the text in the order in which it left John's hands. Thus while the last five verses of chapter xx tell of the final judgement following on the disappearance of the former heaven and the former earth, the first five verses of the next chapter tell, as we should expect, of the new creation, which is to take the place of the old and vanished' creation, that is, the creation of the new heaven and the new earth, the descent of the New Jerusalem from the new heaven to the new earth, and the eternal blessedness of God's people for evermore.

In xxi. 1–5 we have a description of the second Jerusalem, to which I have already drawn your attention.- But we have only the first part of this description, and that in some disorder. For the second and concluding part of it we have to go to verses 3, 4, and 5 of chapter xxii.[1]

This disorder and dislocation are. due to the incompetence of John's editor. For, failing wholly to understand the difference between the two Jerusalems, he compressed them forcibly together, and sought to make one picture out of their conflicting details. In the course of this *tour de force* he inserted the description of the first Jerusalem within that of the second, and to make confusion worse confounded, he prefixed to the description of the first Jerusalem three verses belonging to the Epilogue, i. e. xxi. 6–8. Thus, between the first half of the description of the second or New Jerusalem in xxi. 1–5 and its second half in xxii. 3–5, he has intercalated xxi. 6–8, which belong to the Epilogue of the Book, and xxi. 9–xxii. 2, which describes the first Jerusalem which was to come down to earth to be the seat of Christ's Kingdom. This editor's incompetence for dealing with his master's work is particularly manifest· and offensive here, seeing that he thrusts these twenty-four verses, i.e. xxi. 6–xxii. 2 *between the third and fourth lines of a stanza* which describe God's care for the blessed. The first three lines of this stanza are

Marginal notes: their destruction: next the final judgement, xx. 11–15, which had been initiated by the vanishing into nothingness of the first heaven and the first earth. On the final judgement follows the creation of the new heaven and the new earth and New Jerusalem, xxi. 1–5. But only the first part of the description of the New Jerusalem appears in xxi. 1–5. The rest is found in xxii. 3–5. Explanation of the disordered text. Owing to the editor's ignorance of the essential difference between the two Jerusalems he sought to make one picture of their conflicting details, and intercalated xxi. 6–xxii. 2 between the first half of the description of the New Jerusalem and the second.

---

[1] This fact has already been recognized by Johannes Weiss (*Die Offenbarung*, p. 106 sq.), 1904, but in a very different connexion.

in xxi. 4, but the fourth and concluding line of the stanza is not found till we pass over the next twenty-four verses of the traditional text and come to xxii. 3.

The new Creation. Vision of the New Jerusalem.

Since this description of the new Creation and the blessedness of the righteous therein really closes the Apocalypse, I will place it before you as it ought to be read. But first observe the restored order. This vision follows immediately on that of the final judgement:[1]

xxi. 5ᵃ, 4ᵈ, 5ᵇ, 1–4ᵃᵇᶜ, xxii. 3–5— which forms the real close of the Apocalypse.

xxi. 5ᵃ	And he that sat upon the throne said,
4ᵈ	The former things have passed away;
5ᵇ	Behold I make all things new.

1 And I saw a new heaven and a new earth;
For the first heaven and the first earth had passed away;
And there was no more sea.

2 And the holy city, New Jerusalem, I saw
Coming down out of heaven from God,
Made ready as a bride adorned for her husband.

3 And I heard a great voice from the throne saying,

Behold the tabernacle of God is with men,
And he shall dwell with them,
And they shall be his people,
And he shall be their God.

4ᵃᵇᶜ And God shall wipe away every tear from their eyes,
And death shall be no more,
Neither shall there be mourning nor crying nor pain any more,
xxii. 3ᵃ Neither shall there be any more curse.

xxii. 3ᵇᶜ And the throne of God and the Lamb shall be in it,
And his servants shall serve him,
4 And they shall see his face,
And his name shall be on their foreheads.

5 And there shall be no more night,
And they shall have no need of lamp or light of sun,
For the Lord God shall cause (his face) to shine upon them:
And they shall reign for ever and ever.

[1] For full criticism of this section see my *Commentary*, vol. ii, pp. 200–10, 243–5.

The last four stanzas are the only stanzas of four lines each
in the last three chapters. Such stanzas are found in the
earlier chapters.

This is the real close of the Apocalypse. There is, however, *The Epilogue*
an Epilogue, consisting of thirteen verses, where, though the *consists of God's testi-*
disorder reaches its culminating point, it is yet possible to see *mony to the*
that originally it was composed of three parts, consisting in *truth of the Apocalypse,*
the main of three testimonies to the truth of the Apocalypse, *secondly of*
the first being that given by God, the second that of Christ, *Christ's, and thirdly of*
and the third that of the Seer. Hence the reconstruction here *John's.*
is in the main to be trusted.

This threefold testimony in the Epilogue thus repeats and
confirms the threefold statement made in the Prologue to the
Book in i. 1-3. There it is stated (1) that God Himself gave
the Apocalypse to Christ to make it known to His servants
(i. 1ᵃ—confirmed in xxi. 5ᶜ, 6ᵇ-8); (2) that Christ sent and
made it known through his angel unto John (i. 1ᵇ—confirmed
in xxii. 6-7, 18ᵃ, 16, 13, 12, 10); and (3) that John bare witness
that this Apocalypse was accorded to him by Christ (i. 2—
confirmed in xxii. 3-9, 20-21). The very Beatitude of the
Prologue (i. 3) is taken up and reproduced in the Epilogue in
a slightly different form, xxii. 7: 'Blessed is he that keepeth
the words of the prophecy of this book.'

We have now reconstructed the last three chapters and
undone so far as possible the havoc wrought therein by John's
editor. From this study we naturally conclude that this
editor was a man of mean intelligence. But though he was
lacking in intelligence, he was apparently a better Greek
scholar than his master. For he corrects certain solecistic
constructions of the text in these three chapters (xx. 11,
xxi. 5, 6, xxii. 12), and introduces others which, though
excellent Greek, are against John's usage.[1] But his activities
were not limited to his reconstruction of his master's text
and its occasional correction. He has made certain additions
amounting to about three or four verses. Having now studied
the activities of this editor in the last three chapters, I shall
begin the next lecture with a brief study of his activities in
the first nineteen chapters, where, though not so obvious, they
are generally no less disastrous to the great work of his
master which he undertook to edit.

---

[1] See my *Commentary*, vol. ii, pp. 152, 182; vol. i, p. clviii.

LECTURE II

The disorder
of the tradi-
tional text
of xx–xxii
due to John's
editor.
OUR study of chapters xx–xxii has led to the necessary
hypothesis that these chapters owe their present order to an
editor at the close of the first century. Further, we have
learnt two things regarding this editor. The first is that he
was clearly very ignorant of his master's ideas. The second,
that he was a better Greek scholar than his master, and in
certain cases corrected into normal Greek constructions that
were solecistic and yet specifically Johannine. But the following question naturally suggests itself. If this editor
intervened so drastically in the last three chapters, did he
pass for press—to use a modern expression—the first nineteen
chapters without making any corrections or additions of
his own?

In the earlier chapters of my *Commentary* I adopted the
hypothesis of an editor or of two or more interpolators or
glossers. It was not till I had mastered the problem of
the last three chapters that I recognized that it was one and
the same editor to whom we are indebted for nearly all the
changes and interpolations not only in the last three chapters,
but also in the first nineteen. And in every case where this
editor has intervened he has done so very effectively; for
though he has not added more than twenty verses in the first
nineteen chapters, confusion and darkness have attended un-
failingly on his editorial activities. To a consideration of a
few of these I will now draw your attention, and follow them
up with a brief sketch of the editor's mental and moral outlook.
We find in i. 8 a striking example of his handiwork. This
verse runs: 'I am the Alpha and Omega, saith the Lord God,
which is, and which was, and which is to come, the Almighty.'
This intrusion is singularly infelicitous on three grounds. First,
the context both before and after it is quite unconscious of its
existence. Nay more, no valid explanation of its presence in its
present context has ever been given. But there are stronger
grounds. For, in the second place, the Apocalypse proper has
not yet begun. John has not yet fallen into the visionary
state, and yet he is represented as hearing God speak the
words I have just read. It is not till the tenth verse that
John does fall into a trance, which is described in the words

'I was in the spirit'.[1] Hence if verse 8 is original it must
have occurred in some of the subsequent visions of John. But,
in the third place, when we examine the verse, we recognize
that it could not have been written by John at all. For John
never disconnects the words ὁ θεός ('God') and ὁ παντοκράτωρ [2]
('Almighty') for the good reason that the phrase ὁ θεὸς ὁ
παντοκράτωρ is a stock rendering in the LXX of the O. T.
phrase אלהי הצבאות. In other words 'Almighty' (ὁ παντοκράτωρ)
represents a genitive in the Hebrew dependent on 'God'
(ὁ θεός), and therefore should not be separated as they are
here by eight Greek words. If the words 'which is and
which was and which is to come' are to be combined with the
phrase 'God Almighty', they should be written after them as
they actually are in iv. 8: 'Lord God Almighty, which was
and which is and which is to come'. These words (ὁ θεὸς
ὁ παντοκράτωρ) are never separated in the LXX nor in any work
written in Greek by a Jew, in whose mind the thought of the
original expression still survived. The phrase 'God Almighty'
is found eight times (iv. 8, xi. 17, xv. 3, xvi. 7, 14, xix. 6, 15,
xxi. 22) in our author, and in these ὁ παντοκράτωρ always
follows immediately on ὁ θεός.[3]

Another notable interpolation with a readjustment of the viii. 7–12 an
adjoining context occurs in viii. 7–12. This intrusion, which interpolation.

[1] In my *Commentary*, vol. i, pp. 22, 109–11, I have dealt with this clause
and its significance in Apocalyptic, and on pp. 106 sq. I have given a list
of the many other phrases used in this literature to signify the ecstatic
or trance condition.

[2] ὁ θεὸς (or ὁ κύριος) ὁ παντοκράτωρ occurs as a rendering of this Hebrew
phrase about 120 times in the LXX—in 2 Sam., 1 Kings, 1 Chron.,
Jeremiah, and the Minor Prophets. The latter part of this phrase is
transliterated about 55 times, but this is practically confined to Isaiah,
where it occurs 51 times, and 5 times elsewhere. It is translated
13 times in the Psalms by, κύριος (or θεὸς) τῶν δυνάμεων, and 6 times
elsewhere. This last rendering appears to have been adopted by
Theodotion throughout. Aquila's rendering is κύριος τῶν στρατιῶν, while
Symmachus has both these latter renderings and others. See Thackeray,
Gram. of O. T. Greek, pp. 8 sq.
Occasionally in the LXX we find the word translated with the trans-
literation alongside παντοκράτωρ σαβαώθ. This is probably due to the
incorporation of a marginal gloss.

[3] Some editors—and amongst them Westcott and Hort—insert a comma
between ὁ θεός and ὁ παντοκράτωρ—of course quite wrongly. And all
editors hitherto, so far as I am aware, allow a word to be interpolated
between them in xix. 6, though on the strength of the uncial A, Westcott
and Hort bracket it.

describes the first four Trumpets, is hurtful in every way to
the context. The first four Trumpets are a colourless and
weak reflection of the Seals and Bowls, especially of the

The first
Trumpet
conflicts
with the
fifth Bowl.

latter. The first Trumpet, moreover, conflicts with the fifth.
Thus in the first, 'all the green grass was burnt up' (viii. 7);
in the fifth (ix. 4), it is presupposed to be uninjured. Next,
whereas the order of the words is purely Semitic in the
rest of the chapter, the subject precedes the verb eight times
in these six interpolated verses—an un-Semitic order. Two

Order of
words and
of text and
form of
words against
those of the
Seer.

further peculiarities—not to mention many others—are the
following: In viii. 5, which this editor has re-written, he
represents our author as writing 'thunders and voices and
lightnings'. But our author knows well that the lightnings
always precede the thunders, as we find thrice elsewhere in
the Apocalypse, already in iv. 5, and subsequently in xi. 19,
xvi. 18. But John's editor apparently knew neither this fact
nor his master's usage. viii. 2 he has also re-written. First
of all, having changed the 'three angels', which were to introduce the three demonic plagues, into 'the seven angels', in
order to introduce his enlarged list of seven trumpets, he
next adds οἱ ἐνώπιον τοῦ θεοῦ ἑστήκασιν in order to identify
these seven angels with the well-known seven archangels.
But the Greek form ἑστήκασιν bewrayeth the hand of the
interpolator. Our author never uses the termination -ασιν
for the perfect but -αν. See my *Commentary*, vol. i, p. cxviii.
Further, our author does not use σκοτίζειν as in viii. 12, but
σκοτοῦν (ix. 2, xvi. 10), nor add ἐν with dative after μίγνυσθαι,
as in viii. 7.

But viii. 2 has not only been re-written but transposed from
its original context. In order to recognize this we have only
to observe the order of events which follows on the seventh
(i. e. third) Trumpet in xi. 15, and on the seventh Bowl in
xvi. 17. These events in each case come to a close with
lightnings and thunderings. Between the sounding of this
Trumpet and these lightnings and thunderings and the
pouring forth of this Bowl and like phenomena there is no
intrusive reference to any further fresh visitation. Hence
we infer that, between the opening of the seventh Seal in
viii. 1 and the lightnings and thunderings in viii. 5, there was
originally no intrusive reference to any fresh visitation such
as the Trumpets or Woes, and that viii. 2 stood originally
after viii. 5.

But these are minor evils compared with the great out-

standing one, that this interpolation has, from the days of the
editor at the close of the first century down to the present,
stood between John and his readers, and made the main body
of the Apocalypse a bewildering enigma. It gave birth in These
the third century to that most stultifying of all the methods changes
gave birth
of interpretation, that is, the Recapitulation theory, according of necessity
to the Re-
to which the Seven Seals, the Seven Trumpets, and the Seven capitulation
Bowls deal successively with one and the same series of theory.
events. Furthermore, it is in no slight degree answerable for Made un-
recognizable
the failure of all scholars hitherto to recognize the right the true
significance
meaning of the sealing of the righteous in chapter vii. For of the Sealing
since these four Trumpets usher in physical evils, scholars in vii.
have thereby been misled into the belief that the Sealing in
chapter vii secured the righteous against physical evil. But
a critical investigation of the object of the sealing of the
faithful,[1] from the time of Ezekiel to that of our author,
makes it clear that our author has given a new meaning to
this symbolic action of the sealing of the faithful. The object This sealing
secures the
of the sealing of the righteous on their foreheads in our righteous—
author is not to secure them against *physical* evils, not even not against
physical but
against death itself, but against the demonic powers which begin against
to come into manifestation in ix and against the Satanic powers demonic
evils.
in xii. sq. in the reign of the Antichrist. The words of ix. 4 [2]
can admit of no other meaning. Now this sealing is accom-
plished in vii. Hence the demonic visitations, beginning with
ix, should follow on the sealing without any intervening
physical evils in viii. On the above grounds, therefore, we
excise as an interpolation the first four Trumpets with their
physical evils. There are thus only three Trumpets, and the
sole object of these three Trumpets is to herald the coming
of the three demonic and Satanic Woes.[3]

[1] See my *Commentary*, vol. i, pp. 194–9.
[2] ix. 4. 'And it was said unto them that they should not hurt the
grass of the earth,
    Nor any green thing, nor any tree; but only the men
    That had not the seal of God on their foreheads.'
[3] Accordingly chapter viii should be read as follows, as it stands with
its introduction in my *Commentary*, vol. ii, pp. 407 sq., but without the
foot-notes:
                    CHAPTER VIII
**HEAVEN'S PRAISES STILLED THAT THE PRAYERS OF
    ALL THE FAITHFUL MAY BE PRESENTED TO GOD
    AGAINST THE IMPENDING THREE WOES.**
(1, 3–5, 2 (restored), 6 (restored), 13. Amid the silence of heaven for
the space of half an hour, when all praises and thanksgivings were

Hence the three series of judgements should be designated—
the Seven Seals, the Three Woes, and the Seven Bowls. We
shall in a later lecture recognize the important results which

True inter-
pretation of
viii. 1ᵇ at
last becomes
possible.

flow from this recovery of the original text. When this
interpolation is removed from the text, the true meaning of
the clause ' there was silence in heaven for about the space of
half an hour ' in viii. 1 at once leaps to light after a con-
cealment of over 1800 years. There was silence in heaven
for half an hour, even the praises and thanksgivings of every
order of angels were hushed, until the prayers of all the
saints were presented before God in the verses that follow,

hushed, the prayers of all the saints are presented before God, 1, 3-5, to
shield them in the coming tribulation. Then three Trumpets are given
to three angels, wherewith they prepared to sound, 6, whereupon the
Seer beheld another vision, even an angel flying in mid heaven and
proclaiming, ' Woe, woe, woe to the inhabiters of the earth,' *i. e.* the
non-Christians and faithless, because of the three Woes that were about
to come upon them, 13. On the interpolated passage, viii. 7-12, and the
changes introduced by the interpolator in viii. 1, 2, 6, 13, see notes
below, and vol. i, pp. 219 sqq.)

Silence made
in heaven
that the
prayers of
all the saints
might be
presented
before God,
3-5.

1.   And when he opened the seventh seal, there followed a silence
3.   in heaven for about the space of half an hour.* And another
     angel came and stood by the altar, having a golden censer; and
     there was given to him much incense, that he should offer it
     upon the prayers of all the saints upon the golden altar which
4.   was before the throne. And the smoke of the incense went
     up from the angel's hand before God on behalf of the prayers of
5.   the saints. And the angel took the censer and filled it with the
     fire of the altar, and cast it upon the earth. And there followed
     lightnings, and voices, and thunders, and an earthquake.

Three angels
bidden to
sound the
three
trumpets
announcing
the three
Woes, 2, 6,
13.

2.   And I saw three angels; and unto them were given three
     trumpets.
6.   And the three angels who had the three trumpets prepared
     to sound.
13. And I saw, and I heard an eagle flying in the midst of heaven,
     saying with a loud voice, Woe, woe, woe, to them that dwell
     on the earth, because of the voices of the trumpets of the
     three angels, which are about to sound.

* After the last Seal silence is made in heaven that the prayers of all
the saints may be presented before God, just as after the last Woe
(or Trumpet) come the songs of the Cherubim and Elders xi. 15ᵇ-18,
and after the last Bowl comes the divine voice from the throne in the
temple in heaven. These are the only events that take place between
the last Seal, the last Woe, and the last Bowl, and the lightnings and
thunderings that follow them respectively.

for all the saints were to suffer under the great tribulation about to come upon the earth. Thus assurance is given that God is mindful of His own. It is interesting to note that a remarkable parallel to this statement is found in the Talmud, Chagiga 12ᵇ, where we are told that the companies of angels which sing praises by night in the fifth heaven are silent by day in order that the praises of Israel may be heard.

In chapter xiv there are two most hurtful intrusions, which help us to appraise at their true value the moral and intellectual sides of the editor's character. In xiv. 4 [1] *Interpolation in xiv. 3ᵉ 4ᵃᵇ.* to the description of the 144,000 who follow the Lamb on Mount Zion and bear the name of God and of the Lamb on their foreheads the editor makes the addition, 'These are they who have not defiled themselves with women, for they are virgins'. These interpolated clauses exclude from the 144,000 all women ; for the words 'who have not defiled themselves with women' can only be interpreted of men, and cannot be interpreted of women in any sense whatever, symbolically or metaphorically.

But the range of excluded persons appears greater still. The words 'these are they who have not defiled themselves with women', when taken in connexion with the interpolated words that follow 'for they are virgins', excludes in the opinion

---

[1] There is an interpolated clause also in xiv. 3, but it serves only to introduce the interpolated clauses in xiv. 4. The text xiv. 1-5 should be read as follows :

1. And I saw, and behold the Lamb standing on Mount Zion,
   And with him a hundred and forty and four thousand,
   Having his name and the name of his Father written on their foreheads.

2. And I heard a voice from heaven,
   As the voice of many waters,
   And as the voice of a great thunder.
   And the voice which I heard (was) as (the voice) of harpers

3. Harping with their harps, and singing as it were a new song
   Before the throne, and before the four living creatures and the elders.
   And no one could learn the song
   Save the hundred and forty and four thousand :

4ᶜ. These are they which follow the Lamb whithersoever he goeth.

4ᵈ. These have been redeemed from among men (to be) a sacrifice to God,

5. And in their mouth hath no falsehood been found ;
   For they are blameless.

Proleptic vision of Christ's Kingdom with the glorified martyrs (= 144,000 that were sealed in vii. 4–7) on Mt. Zion in the Millennial period (= vision which comes in its due order in xx. 4–6). The new song sung in heaven and learnt by the 144,000, 2–5.

of some of the best exegetes from the 144,000 all men except those that were strictly celibates. The editor thought that he found here a fit occasion for introducing his ascetic views owing to his misconception of the Greek word ἀπαρχή. He took this word to mean 'the first fruits' or *élite* of the saints, the idea of priority shading off into superiority. Now, if the 144,000 were the *élite* of all the saints, these to his narrow mind could be none other than male celibates. Thus neither St. Peter nor any other married apostle could appear amongst the 144,000. But the word ἀπαρχή has no such meaning here.[1] Nearly three times out of four it means 'sacrifice' or 'gift', and not 'first fruits', in the LXX. In the Greek of our author's time and in the inscriptions in the neighbourhood of Ephesus it was generally used in this sense. Thus the 144,000 are said to be a sacrifice or offering to God as being martyrs. The souls under the altar in vi. 9 are similarly conceived. They were regarded as offered on the heavenly altar.

Interpolator's misconception of the text.

From this interpolation we pass on to another of this editor in xiv. 15-17. Here he reaches the climax of his stupidity. For by the insertion of these verses he has in the first place divided the Messianic Judgement into two acts, the former of which—added by him—is called the harvesting of the earth, xiv. 15-17, and the latter of which is called the vintaging of the earth, xiv. 18-20. In the next place he assigns the former to the Son of Man! and the latter and greater function to an unnamed angel!

The most stupid and hurtful of the editor's interpolations,

Thus the Son of Man or the Messiah is treated as subordinate to or at best as on an equality with an angel—a conception impossible in our author and indeed in Jewish and Christian literature as a whole. But our author never speaks of the judgement as a harvesting of the earth, but as a vintaging, and this vintaging is actually described at length in xix. 11-21, where it is assigned to the Word of God, i.e. the Son of Man, and where it is said of Him that He 'treadeth the winepress of the fierce wrath of God Almighty' (xix. 15). The fact that, notwithstanding this clear appropriation to the Son of Man of the entire Messianic Judgement —described as a vintaging of the earth in xix. 15—this editor could transfer it to an angel, betrays a depth of stupidity all but incomprehensible. He has done more than enough

wherein he makes the Son of Man subordinate to an unnamed angel.

[1] See my *Commentary*, vol. ii, pp. 5-7.

to justify his being branded as a heretic, but no doubt he should be acquitted of this charge on the ground of his hopeless ineptitude. ·

There are many other passages where this editor's intervention has wrought havoc in the work of his master. But time will allow me to notice only one more, and that his closing one, whereby, after that he has taken the most unwarrantable liberties with his author's text by perverting its teaching in some passages and making it absolutely unintelligible in others, he sets the crown on his misdemeanours by invoking an anathema on all such as should in any respect follow the method, which had the sanction of his own example, *The editor's last interpolation.* and either add to or take from the words of the book of this prophecy. Thus in xxii. 18^b–19 he inserts the following anathema, the style of which exhibits several characteristics unlike those of our author : [1]

' If any man shall add unto them,
God shall add unto him the plagues that are written in
   this book.
And if any man shall take away from the words of the
   book of this prophecy,
 God shall take away his part from the tree of life
And out of the holy city, which are written in this book.'

The custom of appending such anathemas began in Deuteronomy in the O. T., and was adopted by many second- and third-rate writers both Jewish and Christian in later times.

Having now done with the editor, though I may occasionally *John's Hebraisms not explicable from the ordinary Greek of his day.* have to recall his work to your notice, I propose to deal with the text, and set before you some of its characteristic Hebraisms and Greek solecisms.

To the Hebraistic character of John's style I first drew attention in lectures delivered before the Universities of Dublin, Oxford, and London. One of the objects of these lectures was to prove the untenableness of the view which was then enforced with great vigour and learning by such scholars as Thumb, Deissmann, and Moulton, that the ordinary Greek of John's day was adequate to explain all the solecisms in his text. Since the publication of these lectures,[2] Dr. Moulton, who alas! perished at sea, owing to the ship in which he was a passenger being torpedoed, accepted the thesis advocated

---

[1] See my *Commentary*, vol. ii, pp. 222-4.
[2] *Studies in the Apocalypse* (second edition).

in these lectures, that John's style cannot be explained save on the supposition that, while he wrote in' Greek, he thought in Hebrew.[1]

On the present occasion I cannot go deeply into this question, but it is possible to give sufficient evidence to prove the intensely Hebraistic character of John's Greek.

The first and most common Hebraism, which occurs nine or ten times, is consistently mistranslated by every version in every language from the second century down to the present day. It is true that here and there the translator, recognizing that certain Greek constructions gave no intelligible sense, abandoned the attempt to translate them literally and reproduced them in the sense suggested by the context. Nearly every ancient version has hit on the right rendering two, three, or four times out of the ten, but modern versions have been less successful in this respect. Their translators have treated the Greek of the Apocalypse as they would that of Xenophon or Thucydides. Hence their renderings of this particular Hebraism have generally ended in disaster. The A. V. is right several times: the R. V. is never right at all.

Now the particular Hebrew idiom so frequently reproduced by John is one constantly recurring in the O. T. It is of the following nature. Hebrew writers after employing the participle often change the construction in what follows, and use finite verbs in subsequent parallel clauses, where logically there should have been participles.

i. 5, 6 a
literal translation of a
Hebrew
idiom.

This idiom first emerges in i. 5–6 τῷ ἀγαπῶντι ἡμᾶς καὶ λύσαντι ἡμᾶς ἐκ τῶν ἁμαρτιῶν ἡμῶν ἐν τῷ αἵματι αὐτοῦ καὶ ἐποίησεν ἡμᾶς βασιλείαν. Here ἐποίησεν is a Hebraism for

---

[1] Moulton (Peake's *Commentary on the Bible*) writes: 'Dr. R. H. Charles has recently shown how many of its (i. e. of Revelation) mannerisms are due to the literal transference of Semitic idioms' (p. 592). And again: 'Mark and Revelation might have been equally telling in the Semitic tongue, from which they were virtually translated' (p. 593). Such may be regarded as the accepted view of scholars on this subject now. To show what a revolutionary change of opinion has come about in the last six years it is only necessary to quote a statement from Moulton's *Grammar* (i, pp. 9 sq.)—the most brilliant grammar that has ever appeared on the Greek Testament—where he categorically declares: 'Even the Greek of the Apocalypse itself does not seem to owe any of its "blunders" to Hebraism.' I have always found that the greatest scholars are the readiest to withdraw their mistaken views or acknowledge their errors on the production of evidence, but with second-rate and third-rate scholars my experience has been very different.

ποιήσαντι, and one late uncial and many cursives have actually so corrected the text and several of the ancient versions which have here been followed by the A. V. The scribes of the manuscripts had of course no idea of the Hebraism underlying the text, but they felt and felt rightly that ἐποίησεν could not be construed as good Greek nor as good sense. But the Revised Version refused to deal so cavalierly with the Greek before them. In the face of the evidence of the manuscripts and versions there could be no doubt as to ἐποίησεν being the correct text. Hence, since the Revisers knew nothing about the Hebraism here, they translated the Greek before them literally, as follows: 'Unto him that loveth us and loosed us from our sins by his blood; And *he made us* to be a kingdom . . .; To him be the glory and the dominion for ever and ever.' Now in the first place this rendering is not English; and its bad English cannot be got over by mispunctuating the text as most editors do. Westcott, Hort, and Swete seek to evade the difficulty by treating the clause καὶ ἐποίησεν . . . πατρὶ αὐτοῦ as a parenthesis while others like Moffatt treat it as an anacoluthon. If this were the only passage in our author where this peculiar construction occurred, such explanations would be quite justified, but it will not do in our author. We have here the same Hebrew idiom, which recurs later in eight passages. Accordingly the passage is to be translated:

Unto him that loveth us and hath loosed us from our sins by his blood
And *made* us to be a kingdom, priests unto his God and Father—
Unto him be the glory and the dominion for ever and ever.'

Its right translation.

Again in i. 18 the failure to recognize this idiom in ὁ ζῶν καὶ ἐγενόμην νεκρός has led the Revisers and most scholars to mispunctuate and mistranslate the text, and some scholars as Haussleiter, Wellhausen, and Moffatt, with certain Latin versions all of which probably go back to one Greek manuscript,[1] to excise a phrase indispensable to the text. The Revisers render: 'Fear not; I am the first and the last, and *the Living one; and I was dead*, and behold I am alive for evermore, and I have the keys of death and of Hades.' i. 17ᶜ–19 should

i. 18 wrongly translated hitherto.

[1] See my *Commentary*, vol. ii, pp. 453–4; vol. i, p. clxxxi.

be rendered as verse and either as three distichs, or as two tristichs, the first of which runs as follows:

> 'Fear not; I am the first and the last:
> And *he that was alive and died*,[1] and behold I am alive for evermore;
> And have the keys of death and of Hades.'

[1] When Dr. Burney called my attention orally to the fact that the Hebrew idiom, which I presupposed as underlying i. 18, did not admit of the rendering which I had given it, i. e. 'And he that liveth and was dead', I welcomed the correction, and informed him at the same time that his criticism enabled me at last to see the true sense of the passage: i.e. 'And he that was alive and died.' I find that Dr. Burney has since dealt with this subject in the *J. T. S.*, pp. 371-6, July, 1921, where he accepts all my presuppositions of a certain Hebraism save two—i. e. in i. 18, xx. 4. As regards i. 18, he maintains that the right translation of the passage is that of the R.V.:

'Fear not; I am the first and the last and the Living one: and I was dead, and behold, I am alive for evermore.'

But no reasonable doubt can exist as to the wrongness of the R.V. here, when we bring to the investigation a knowledge of the author's usage. In the first place the ὁ ζῶν is not to be connected with the preceding words—ἐγώ εἰμι ὁ πρῶτος καὶ ὁ ἔσχατος—as I have shown in my *Commentary*. These words express a conception complete in itself as in ii. 8, xxii. 13; Isaiah xli. 4, xliv. 6, xlviii. 12. Even in Semitic prose the expression 'I am the first and the last and the Living one' would be an extraordinary one. But the main and conclusive ground for the translation, which I have given above in the text, is as follows. The name of Christ is modelled on that of God in i. 4, iv. 8. Now in these two passages we have a definition of God given in three time-determinations ὁ ἦν καὶ ὁ ὢν καὶ ὁ ἐρχόμενος (iv. 8; in i. 4 the order is different but the context accounts for the variation). Similarly, in that of Christ with its three time-determinations we have the nearest approach possible to this in:

> ὁ ζῶν καὶ ἐγενόμην νεκρός,
> καὶ ἰδοὺ ζῶν εἰμὶ εἰς τ. αἰῶνας τ. αἰώνων.

But this is not all. As the name of Christ is modelled on that of God, *so the name of the Antichrist is modelled on that of Christ*. Thus in xvii. 8 the Antichrist is twice mentioned, and each time the title ascribed to him recalls that of Christ. The first is:

> ἦν καὶ οὐκ ἔστιν καὶ μέλλει ἀναβαίνειν ἐκ τῆς ἀβύσσου,

and the second:

> ὅ τι ἦν καὶ οὐκ ἔστιν καὶ πάρεσται·

The triple time-designation of Christ, therefore, in i. 18 refers to three distinct periods: His eternal past (ὁ ζῶν—'He that was alive': cf. in the preceding line ἐγώ εἰμι ὁ πρῶτος), the hour of His death, and His eternal future. The ὁ ζῶν could as a Hebraism mean either 'He that was (or "had been") alive', or 'He that liveth', or 'He that is about to live' (cf. Kautzsch's *Gesenius' Heb. Gram.*, § 116 d). The context in i. 18

The next passage which I shall bring before you is in ii. 23 hitherto wrongly translated.
ii. 23 ὁ ἐραυνῶν ... καὶ δώσω. Here the failure of scholars

can admit only of the first. For our author's Hebraistic use of this Greek
participle as equivalent to a past participle see xv. 2 τοὺς νικῶντας ἐκ τοῦ
θηρίου, 'those that had been victorious over the beast', and vii. 14
οἱ ἐξερχόμενοι, ' those that had come out '.

How easy it is to fall into an error such as I have been guilty of in
i. 18 can be illustrated from the fact that Dr. Burney has fallen into
the very same error twice in the very article in the J. T. S. where
he has dealt with mine in Rev. i. 18. It is quite true that he was misled
by Driver as I was myself. But Driver's error calls for slight criticism.
He was a pioneer in his *Hebrew Tenses*, and had not yet recognized the
fact that, though the participle followed in a subsequent clause with ו
(vav consecutive) and a finite verb (in the imperfect) may in all cases be
taken as equivalent to vav with sheva and the perfect when these are
separated by one or more words, *the converse is not always true*, though
Driver obviously implies this. To this fact we shall return presently.

Returning now to Dr. Burney's article in the J. T. S. (p. 373) we find
that Dr. Burney has quoted from Driver's *Hebrew Tenses*[3], § 117, three
passages from Isaiah, i. e. xiv. 17, xxx. 2, xliii. 7, as examples of the
resolution of the participle into a finite verb in the following clause,
where according to this idiom *the action expressed by the finite verb should
express the proper sequence of the action expressed by the participle.*
Dr. Burney writes, and the italics are his : ' We do *not* find cases in
which the sequence describes an event *actually prior in time to its
antecedent.*' This being so, xxx. 2 (ההלכים לרדת מצרים ופי לא שאלו)
is wrongly assigned to this category by Dr. Burney in the body of his
article, but later recognizing this fact, he withdraws xxx. 2 as an example
of this idiom in a foot-note at the close of his article, and treats the clause
with the finite verb as a circumstantial clause. But just as certainly
Dr. Burney should have recognized that neither could xliii. 7 be regarded
as an example of this idiom, and be translated as 'Everyone that is called
(הנקרא) and whom I have created' (ולכבודי בראתיו). Here the act of
creation is antecedent to the act of calling. Hence, however we explain
xliii. 7, it cannot be brought under this idiom. If it were an example of
this idiom, it would be, as we know, the equivalent of כל הנקרא בשמי
ואבראהו לכבודי—a thing of no meaning. In the grammatical explanation
of xiv. 17, xxx. 2, xliii. 7 Dr. Burney has followed Driver (*Hebrew
Tenses*[3]) in the text of his article, but, as I have shown, abandoned his
guidance in the closing note in the case of xxx. 2. But Dr. Burney must
also abandon Driver's guidance in Isa. xiv. 17 שם תבל כמדבר ועריו הרם.
Since according to Dr. Burney the latter of these two clauses is the
equivalent of ויהרם עריו, the action expressed by the finite verb must
express the proper sequence of (but in no case an action prior to) the
action expressed by the participle. Yet he translates it as follows : 'that
made the world a wilderness and overthrew the cities thereof.' But the
desolation of the world follows upon, but does not precede, the destruction

to recognize the Hebraism behind these words has led to
a misinterpretation of the text. Owing to the future verb
of its cities. There is yet another example in Isaiah to which Professor
Buchanan Gray has drawn my attention, and to which I shall return.

Explanations, therefore, of Isa. xiv. 17, xliii. 7 must be found other
than those given by Dr. Burney. In the text of his article in the
J. T. S. he has interpreted the Hebrew in Isa. xiv. 17, xxx. 2, xliii. 7
in the same way that I interpreted the Hebrew idiom, which I presupposed as underlying Rev. i. 18, and to which he rightly objected. But
the same error is implied in Driver's *Hebrew Tenses*, which is the most
original work on this subject. See Note on p. 76.

Grammatically xiv. 17, xliii. 7 could be explained as circumstantial
clauses, but this explanation is unsatisfactory. Professor Buchanan
Gray holds that in both passages we have *parallel and not consecutive
clauses.* The parallelism is alternate. This same construction—a fact to
which Professor Gray drew my attention—is found in xlviii. 1 הנקראים
בשם ישראל וממי יהודה יצאו. Here the last clause cannot be re-written
as ויצאו ממי יהודה any more than in xiv. 17, xliii. 7. Professor Gray,
accordingly, distinguishes *between the participle followed by ו and
the imperfect and the participle followed by ו and the perfect with one or
more words intervening,* and he rightly insists that, though the former
construction can always be replaced by the latter, the converse, though
generally, is not always possible. Here a distinct advance is made in
Hebrew syntax.

To sum up the results of what we have arrived at so far. My rendering
of Rev. i. 18 is wrong, but as regards the Hebrew idiom I presuppose in
i. 18 I am right, though my rendering of it must be corrected as I
have shown.

Again, Dr. Burney objects to my excision of οἵτινες as an addition
of John's editor in Rev. xx. 4 and also to my rendering of Rev. xx. 4.
But inasmuch as *our author never elsewhere follows up the participle
with καί and a relative clause,* but in accordance with a Hebrew idiom
omits the relative, I have bracketed the οἵτινες as an interpolation.
Here Dr. Burney makes another suggestion, which is possible, but
unnecessary, and which I am unable to accept. How then are we to
explain xx. 4 τῶν πεπελεκισμένων διὰ τ. μαρτυρίαν Ἰησοῦ καὶ διὰ τ. λόγον τ.
θεοῦ καὶ [οἵτινες] οὐ προσεκύνησαν τὸ θηρίον οὐδὲ τ. εἰκόνα αὐτοῦ, καὶ οὐκ
ἔλαβον τὸ χάραγμα κτλ. There are two probable ways. 1. First of all we
observe that in vi. 9 τῶν ἐσφαγμένων διὰ τὸν λόγον τοῦ θεοῦ καὶ διὰ τὴν
μαρτυρίαν ἣν εἶχον refers to the martyrs under Nero. These were martyred
διὰ τ. λόγον τ. θεοῦ καὶ διὰ τ. μαρτυρίαν ἣν εἶχον. But in xx. 4 the martyrdoms referred to are those that the Seer expected would take place under
Domitian, and the Seer carefully distinguishes the grounds of the Domitianic persecution from those of the Neronic. The first grounds he advances
are the same in the Domitianic persecution (διὰ τ. μαρτυρίαν Ἰησοῦ καὶ διὰ
τ. λόγον τ. θεοῦ) as in the Neronic (διὰ τ. λόγον τ. θεοῦ καὶ διὰ τ. μαρτυρίαν
ἣν εἶχον). But there are further grounds advanced for the martyrdoms
under Domitian. Hence these grounds καὶ οὐ προσεκύνησαν τὸ θηρίον κτλ.
are simply parallel—not to the participial clause preceding—but only

(δώσω) this passage has always hitherto been taken as referring to the final judgement, and has therefore been misinterpreted. But as the context shows, it should refer to God's present judgements, and the Hebraism here admits of no other translation. The universal and wrong rendering of this passage hitherto has been:

'Behold I do cast her into a bed, and them that commit adultery with her into great tribulation ... And I will kill her children with death. And all the churches shall know that I am he which searcheth the reins and the hearts: and *I will give* unto each one of you according to your works.'

Instead of this rendering which does such wrong to the original, we should translate as follows and in verse:

'Behold I will cast her upon a bed of suffering,
　And those that commit adultery with her into great tribulation;
And her children I will slay with pestilence:

to the prepositional clause διὰ τ. μαρτυρίαν 'Ιησοῦ καὶ διὰ τ. λόγον τ. θεοῦ. In that case we have exactly the same idiom as in Ezekiel xxxvi. 18: 'I poured out my fury upon them because of the blood (עַל הַדָּם) which they had poured out upon the land and because they had defiled it with their idols' (וּבְגִלּוּלֵיהֶם טִמְּאוּהָ). Here the verbal clause ('because they had defiled' &c.) is parallel to the prepositional clause ('because of the blood') just as in Rev. xx. 4. Aquila and Theodotion render in Greek such as that of John the Seer περὶ τοῦ αἵματος οὗ ἐξέχεαν ἐν τῇ γῇ καὶ ἐν τοῖς εἰδώλοις αὐτῶν ἐμίαναν αὐτήν. Accordingly we should render xx. 4^{e-h}:

'And ⟨I saw⟩ the souls of them that had been beheaded because of the witness of Christ,
And because of the word of God,
And because they had not worshipped the beast
Nor yet his image,
Nor received his mark upon their forehead
And upon their hand.'

2. Or xx. 4^{e-h} may be taken as a combination of parallel clauses (participle in first clause with finite verb in second) in the same way that we must take Isa. xiv. 17, xliii. 7, xlviii. 1. In that case we should translate the second distich as follows:

'And that had not worshipped the beast
Nor yet his image.'

No. 1 is probably to be preferred. In bringing this note to a close, I may observe that some expositors maintain that there are two classes of the faithful referred to here—martyrs and confessors. But such an interpretation requires us to take ἔζησαν at the close of xx. 4 as bearing *simultaneously* two meanings—'came to life again' and 'continued to live'!

The above note has been submitted to Professor Buchanan Gray and Dr. Cowley, and to its conclusions they both give their suffrages, the former as an actual contributor, and the latter as a Hebrew critic.

And so all the Churches shall know
That I am he that searcheth the reins and hearts,
And *giveth* to each one of you according to your works.'

I will next draw your attention to two mistranslations of our author, where, owing to their failure to recognize this particular idiom beneath the Greek, the translators have introduced into their translations a breach in the unity of time, which does not belong to the original. In xiv. 2-3 we have the Greek :

Καὶ ἡ φωνὴ ἣν ἤκουσα ὡς κιθαρῳδῶν
κιθαριζόντων ἐν ταῖς κιθάραις αὐτῶν. 3 Καὶ ᾄδουσιν.

Here the Revised and practically every version renders:

' And the voice which I heard was as the voice of harpers harping with their harps: *and they sing.*' But when once we have recognized the Hebraism in the text, we see that there is only one rendering of the text possible and that this is:

' And the voice which I heard was as the voice of harpers
Harping with their harps *and singing.*'

Similarly in xv. 2-3 instead of the wrong rendering, ' I saw them that were victorious . . . standing by the sea of glass, having the harps of God and *they sing,*' we should render, ' And I saw . . . them that had been victorious . . . standing by the sea of glass, having the harps of God, and *singing.*'

So much for this Hebraism which recurs so frequently in our author.

xii. 7—the
hopeless
crux of
scholars in
the past—
is a literal
rendering of
a well-known
Hebrew
idiom.
I can only deal with one or two more of the many Hebraisms in our author. In xii. 7 we have a classical Hebrew idiom rendered literally into Greek. Considered, however, from the standpoint of Greek grammar, it is at once impossible and unintelligible, and so it has proved a hopeless *crux* to Greek scholars and grammarians from the second century down to the present day. This idiom which I shall explain presently, recurs twice in xiii. 10, but only in one manuscript, i.e. A. In the remaining six uncials and all the cursives this unintelligible Greek has been removed from the text and the text emended in various ways. We have here a priceless testimony to the unique excellence of the text of codex A in

the Apocalypse. Let us now return to xii. 7, where the Greek runs as follows:

Καὶ ἐγένετο πόλεμος ἐν τῷ οὐρανῷ,
ὁ Μιχαὴλ καὶ οἱ ἄγγελοι αὐτοῦ τοῦ πολεμῆσαι μετὰ τοῦ δράκοντος.

Every modern grammarian of the N. T. has had his fling at this passage from Weiss and Blass to Moulton and Robertson, but they have all alike failed to explain it, and not a single scholar of any country or period has recognized the recurrence of this same idiom in xiii. 10, where, it is true, it is preserved only in the uncial A. The *crux* of this passage is, of course, τοῦ πολεμῆσαι. It may at once be acknowledged that it is impossible to explain it from the Greek grammar of any period. Accordingly it has never yet been rightly translated into any language from the second century to the present. But the Hebrew scholar who studies the Apocalypse should not experience any insuperable difficulty in this passage, and so we find a partial explanation of it in Ewald and Bleek. They recognized that τοῦ πολεμῆσαι was a Hebraism, but they did not attempt to deal with the nominatives ὁ Μιχαὴλ καὶ οἱ ἄγγελοι αὐτοῦ which precede the infinitive. Some acquaintance with the LXX would have solved this further difficulty. In fact we find in the LXX the construction of the nominative with the infinitive several times, where it is the literal reproduction of a pure Hebraism. In Hosea ix. 13 we have Ἐφράιμ τοῦ ἐξαγαγεῖν, a literal rendering of אפרים להוציא, 'Ephraim must bring forth'; in Eccles. iii. 15, we have the extraordinary Greek sentence, ὅσα τοῦ γίνεσθαι ἤδη γέγονεν, a literal rendering of אשר להיות כבר היה, 'What shall be hath already been'. In both cases the Hebrew is excellent but the Greek is impossible. It is the literal rendering of a very technical Hebrew idiom. It is only by retranslating it into Hebrew that we can translate it at all. In like manner we must re-translate our text into Hebrew. The Hebrew would run thus:

וַתְּהִי מִלְחָמָה בַּשָּׁמַיִם
מִיכָאֵל וּמַלְאָכָיו לְהִלָּחֵם בַּתַּנִּין .

Hence we translate:

'There was war in heaven.
Michael and his angels had to fight with the Dragon.'

The right translation of xii. 7.

The idea is a most vivid one. Satan and his angels had been cast down from heaven. Mustering his forces anew, Satan returns to the attack and strives to storm the ramparts of heaven. Here he and his armies are met by Michael and his angels and hurled down again to the earth. In the strong and vivid words of our text we have :

> ' There was war in heaven :
> Michael and his angels had to fight with the dragon ;
> And the dragon fought and his angels and he prevailed not,
> Neither was their place found any more in heaven.'

Of the many other Hebraisms I will deal only with one more. We find that when Hebrew and Greek words agree as to their primary meanings, the secondary meanings of the Hebrew words are in a few cases unwittingly and quite wrongly assigned to the Greek. Thus in x. 1 we have the extraordinary phrase οἱ πόδες αὐτοῦ ὡς στύλοι πυρός. Now it is clear that πόδες cannot have its Greek meaning here. Our author cannot say of an angel : ' His face was as the sun and his *feet* were as pillars of fire !' This would be an extraordinary simile. Feet like pillars of fire ! There must be some error here, and the source of the error at once leaps to light, if we reflect that the Hebrew word for 'foot' (רגל) can also mean ' leg'. This word means either foot or leg also in Aramaic and Arabic. Moreover, we find that in the LXX the secondary meaning of the Hebrew word is already, as in our text, assigned to the Greek word as in Isa. vii. 20 (שׁער הרגלים = τὰς τρίχας τῶν ποδῶν). Here πούς must be rendered ' leg', though this Greek word never means ' leg' in ordinary Greek.

I cannot dwell longer on the Hebraistic character of John's style, but must now bring before you a few of the many Greek solecisms in our author.

The following remarkable constructions with ἐπί are peculiar to our author. When our author uses ἐπί with some case of θρόνος, νεφέλη, or ἵππος, the case of these words is determined by the case of the preceding participle καθήμενος. When this participle is in the nominative or accusative, ἐπί is followed by the accusative of these words; when the participle is in the genitive, ἐπί is followed by the genitive of these words; when the participle is in the dative, ἐπί is followed by the dative of these words. Thus we have :

(α) ὁ καθήμενος   ⎧ ἐπὶ τὸν θρόνον.
    (or)   ⎨ ἐπὶ τὴν νεφέλην.
 τὸν καθήμενον[1] ⎩ ἐπὶ τὸν ἵππον.

                   ⎧ ἐπὶ τοῦ θρόνου.
(β) τοῦ καθημένου ⎨ ἐπὶ τοῦ ἵππου.
                   ⎩ ἐπὶ ὑδάτων.

(γ) τῷ καθημένῳ   ἐπὶ τῷ θρόνῳ.

These hard-and-fast syntactical forms of our author are not observed by his editor. He prefers to use ἐπί with the genitive no matter what may be the case of the preceding participle, and undoubtedly he is the better Grecian in so doing. Thus he runs counter to our author's practice in seven passages, and corrects our author's usage in xx. 11, and probably in vii. 15, ix. 17. In the addition he makes in xiv. 15–17 he uses ἐπί with the genitive twice in this construction against our author's usage. *(margin: John's editor corrects some of these solecisms.)*

In this connexion I may add three more out of the many cases where the editor has shown his ignorance of his master's style. In xxii. 12 the non-Johannine order of the text ὡς τὸ ἔργον ἐστὶν αὐτοῦ seems due to the editor; for John never separates the genitive possessive pronoun from its noun in the 300 passages where it occurs. Hence if the phrase is John's it must have originally run: ὡς τὸ ἔργον αὐτοῦ ἐστίν. Again, our author never uses ἐπὶ τὴν γῆν, but ἐπὶ τῆς γῆς or εἰς τὴν γῆν. But in the interpolated passage in xiv. 16 we find ἐπὶ τὴν γῆν. Another non-Johannine expression κράζων ἐν φωνῇ μεγάλῃ occurs in this verse. John omits the ἐν in this phrase. The following expressions are hopelessly ungrammatical from the standpoint of Greek syntax, and yet they are deliberately chosen by our author, and his reasons for his choice of some of them are not wholly hidden from us: *(margin: Other solecisms.)*

i. 4 ἀπὸ ὁ ὤν.
iv. 8 ὁ ἦν καὶ ὁ ὢν καὶ ὁ ἐρχόμενος.
i. 13, xiv. 14 ὅμοιον υἱὸν ἀνθρώπου.
ii. 1 τῷ ἀγγέλῳ τῷ ἐν Ἐφέσῳ ἐκκλησίας.

The last solecism occurs at the beginning of the seven epistles to the Churches in ii–iii. I will spend a few minutes *(margin: The astounding solecism τῷ ἀγγέλῳ τῷ ἐν ... ἐκκλησίας.)*

[1] This usage is against the reading in xiv. 6: τοὺς καθημένους ἐπὶ τῆς γῆς (ℵC 025. 046 s¹ Pr gig vg). In such a combination in our author we should expect ἐπὶ τὴν γῆν. Hence ℵ 051 s² Tyc is to be preferred here: τοὺς κατοικοῦντας ἐπὶ τῆς γῆς.

on this interesting construction. The grammatical Greek construction here is of course τῷ ἀγγέλῳ τῆς ἐν Ἐφέσῳ ἐκκλησίας.

Naturally the scribes objected strongly to such a solecism as τῷ ἀγγέλῳ τῷ ἐν Ἐφέσῳ ἐκκλησίας. Thus it has been corrected out of all the uncial manuscripts but two, and out of all the cursives but three. In the cursives it has survived only in one of the seven passages in each of the cursives, and only once in the uncial C. In the Codex Alexandrinus it survives three times out of the seven. And this illegitimate correction of the scribes has so influenced editors of the Greek text that only Griesbach and Lachmann in Germany nearly a hundred years back, and Hort in England, have had at once the discernment to recognize the reading of A as original and the courage to adopt it. And yet this abnormal construction is undoubtedly Johannine. For an examination of his entire text shows that he avoids inserting a prepositional phrase between *the article and its noun* though he has no objection to a prepositional phrase between the article and a participle : in other words, that John deliberately avoids such a construction as τῆς ἐν Ἐφέσῳ ἐκκλησίας. Now it is all the more creditable to the above three scholars that they adopted the reading of A, although they knew nothing about John's idiosyncrasy in regard to this construction. From an exhaustive examination of the versions, I can further prove that, though the Greek manuscripts only preserve the original text in four out of the seven passages, the right text is supported in all the seven passages by one, two, three, or more of the ancient versions.[1] Thus the original form of the text in these passages has passed from the region of the probable into that of actual fact. This is of course a question of pure scholarship and one that does not affect the sense. But it is none the less important on that account. Before we can master John's style we must recover so far as we can the form of the text as it left his hand. Moreover, this solecism becomes a criterion for determining the value of manuscripts and versions.

I have now dealt at sufficient length for our present purposes with John's abounding Hebraisms and unique Greek Grammar. These mark off his style from that of every other Greek writer from the time of Homer to the present.

[1] See my *Commentary*, vol. ii, p. 244.

The next feature that characterizes John's style is his Poetical frequent use of the poetical parallelism we find in Hebrew parallelism —feature of poetry. Though he has for his theme the inevitable conflicts John's style. and antagonisms of good and evil, of God and the powers of darkness, yet his Book is emphatically a Book of Songs.

Of the twenty-two chapters of which the Book is composed, there are only four that are completely prose. In the remaining eighteen we find at times short songs, at others almost the entire text is cast into this poetic form. Nearly always when dealing with his greatest themes the Seer's words assume consciously or perhaps at times unconsciously a poetic form. To print such passages as prose is to rob them of half their force. And it is not only the form that is thereby lost, but also much of the thought that in a variety of ways is reinforced by the parallelism.

Before I quote these passages in the form in which they This fact is should be given, I wish to emphasize the help that the recog- valuable as nition of this poetical element in our author renders in the a canon of criticism of the text. I will give a few illustrations of its criticism— value in determining the text of our author. as in xxi. 3–4^{abc}, xxii. 3–5.

As the first illustration of the value of the poetical form in The poetic the criticism of the text, I will place before you our author's form fur- description of the New Jerusalem. In this description— nishes almost xxi. 3–4$^{a b c}$, xxii. 3–5, which I print below—you will observe demonstra- that in the traditional order of the text, due to John's editor, tive evidence as to the twenty-four verses have been introduced between the third immediate and fourth lines of the second stanza. Thus when we have sequence of read the first three lines of this second stanza, i. e. xxii. 3-5 on xxi. 4^{abc}.

xxi. 4$^{a b c}$ 'And God shall wipe away every tear from their eyes,
          And death shall be no more,
          Neither shall there be mourning nor crying nor pain
             any more.'

We look in vain for the fourth line until we have got through twenty-four verses which have nothing to do with this poem or its subject. Then at last we come on the missing line

xxii. 3^{a} 'Neither shall there be any more curse.'

Thereupon follow the next two stanzas which complete this poem. Thus the poetical form is here in itself decisive of the original order of this section of the text. But this evidence does not stand alone. As I have shown in my *Commentary* (vol. ii, p. 153), a certain collocation of Greek words which occurs three times in xxi. 1–4, recurs twice in xxii. 3–5, and nowhere else throughout our author, or in the rest of the New Testament. This can hardly be accidental. Furthermore, the subject-matter of the poem coheres so perfectly together that its evidence taken with what precedes amounts to demonstration.

Although portions of this great poem have already been given, its simplicity, beauty, and sublimity can be best appreciated by being placed before you as a whole:

xxi. 5[a] 'And he that sat upon the throne said,
   4[d] The former things have passed away;
   5[b] Behold I make all things new.

   1   And I saw a new heaven and a new earth;
        For the first heaven and the first earth had passed
          away;
        And there was no more sea.

   2   And the holy city, New Jerusalem, I saw
        Coming down out of heaven from God,
        Made ready as a bride adorned for her husband.

   3   And I heard a great voice from the throne saying,

        Behold the tabernacle of God is with men,
        And he shall dwell with them,
        And they shall be his people,
        And he shall be their God.

   4[abc] And God shall wipe away every tear from their eyes,
        And death shall be no more,
        Neither shall there be mourning nor crying nor pain
          any more,
xxii. 3[a] Neither shall there be any more curse.

xxii. 3[bc] And the throne of God and the Lamb shall be in it,
        And his servants shall serve him.
   4   And they shall see his face,
        And his name shall be on their foreheads.

   5   And there shall be no more night,
        And they shall have no need of lamp or light of sun,
        For the Lord God shall cause (his face) to shine upon
          them:
        And they shall reign for ever and ever.'

The next illustration comes from chapter ii. Here the Epistle to the Church of Thyatira (ii. 18–29) consists of ten stanzas, eight of which consist of three lines each. That the fifth consists of three lines also and not of four as it is in the

manuscripts, we should naturally presume from the fact that
the four stanzas before it and the two immediately after it
are three-line stanzas.   And this presumption is confirmed by
the fact that the additional line in the fifth stanza contains
a non-Johannine construction, and is also against the right
sense of the context.   Hence the clause 'unless they repent
of their works' is to be omitted, and the stanza to be read as
follows :

> ii. 22 'Behold I will cast her upon a bed of suffering,
>   And those that commit adultery with her into great
>   tribulation,
> 23   And her children I will slay with pestilence.' [1]

(marginal note: ii. 22-3, where a clause has been interpolated.)

Of the ten stanzas, nine thus consist of three lines each.   This
being so, it is highly probable therefore that the eighth stanza,
which consists of only two lines in the manuscript, has lost a
line.   That the text has suffered here at the hands of the
editor or of careless copyists, we see from the last two stanzas,
where a line belonging to the tenth stanza has been transposed
into the ninth.   These should, of course, be read as follows :

> ii. 26 'And he that overcometh, even he that keepeth my
>   works unto the end—
>   To him will I give authority over the nations :
> 27c   As I also have received from my Father ;
>
> 27a   And he shall break them with a rod of iron ;
>   b   As potters' vessels shall they be dashed in pieces :
> 28   And I will give him the morning star.'

(marginal note: ii. 26-8, where a line has been transposed.)

This restoration is confirmed by a comparison of iii. 21 :

> 'To him that overcometh, I will grant to sit with me
>   on my throne,
> As I also have overcome, and sat down with my
>   Father on his throne.'

Next the opening vision in chap. xiv of the 144,000 glorified
martyrs on Mount Zion would consist of five stanzas of three
lines each, but for a prosaic addition [2] in the fourth stanza,
which destroys entirely the verse structure.   But we find on
exegetical grounds (see above, p. 27 sq.), independently of the
verse structure that we are obliged to excise 3e, 4a b.   Thus

(marginal note: xiv. 2-4. Here the critical results arrived at on independent grounds are confirmed by the verse structure.)

---

[1] See my *Commentary*, vol. ii, p. 392, notes 4 and 5.

[2] xiv. 3e 4a b, 'Who were redeemed from the earth. These are they
who were not defiled with women ; for they are virgins.'

the thought and the form combine in requiring the excision of these clauses and so we read:

xiv. 2ᵈ 'And the voice which I heard was as the voice of harpers

3ᵃᵇᶜᵈ Harping with their harps and singing as it were a new song
Before the throne and before the four living creatures and the elders.

And no one could learn that song
Save the hundred and forty and four thousand:

4ᶜᵈ These are they which follow the lamb whithersoever he goeth.

5   These have been redeemed from amongst men to be a sacrifice to God,
And in their mouth hath no falsehood been found;
For they are blameless.'

xix. 11–16.
Here the verse-structure requires the excision of 12ᶜ—a conclusion necessary on other grounds.

In xix. 11–16 we have a vision of the Divine Warrior written in eight stanzas of two lines each. But at the end of the third stanza all the manuscripts insert a third line 12ᶜ 'having a name written which no man knoweth save he himself'. The form of the adjoining stanzas raises the presumption that this third line is an intrusion, and this presumption is confirmed by three facts: first, this addition forms an anacoluthon. Secondly, it breaks the connexion of thought. We do not expect a reference to the name in the midst of a description of the person and dress. Thirdly, it is contradicted by the next stanza, where the Divine Warrior's name is declared to be 'the Word of God'. Hence we read:

xix. 11 'And I saw the heaven opened;
And behold a white horse.

And he that sat thereon—Faithful and True;
And in righteousness doth he judge and make war.

12ᵃᵇ And his eyes are as a flame of fire,
And on his head are many diadems.

13   And he is clothed with a garment dipped in blood,
And his name is called the Word of God.'

xx. 4–6 in their restored order.

As another illustration of the critical value of the form of the text I will give the vision of the kingdom of Christ and the glorified martyrs in xx. 4–6. This vision would consist of seven stanzas of two lines each, but for the prosaic addition in the fifth stanza xx. 5ᵃ: 'The rest of the dead lived not till

the thousand years were fulfilled.'[1]   If this were original we
should expect it to be introduced by a conjunction and that
an adversative one: 'And they lived and reigned with Christ
a thousand years, but the rest of the dead lived not.'

But no such conjunction is given.   Hence the words appear
to be a marginal gloss incorporated in the text.   Moreover, it
intervenes between two lines which should not be separated ;
for the second line (' This is the first resurrection ') defines what
the first line means.   Thus the fifth stanza should be read :

xx. 4[i] 'And they lived and reigned with Christ a thousand
                years :
     5[b]   This is the first resurrection.'

Thus xx. 4-6 should be read as follows :

xx. 4-6. (Vision of the glorified martyrs who reign with
Christ for a thousand years.)

4[c-h] 'And ⟨I saw⟩ the souls of them that had been beheaded
                because of the witness of Christ,
           And because of the word of God,

           And because [2] they had not worshipped the beast,
           Nor yet his image,

           Nor had received his mark upon their forehead
           And upon their hand.

4[a b]   And I saw thrones, and they seated themselves thereon,
           And judgement was given unto them.[3]

4[i]   And they lived and reigned with Christ a thousand
                years.

5[b]   This is the first resurrection.

6   Blessed and holy is he that hath part in the first
                resurrection :
           Over these the second death hath no power ;

           But they shall be priests of God and of Christ,
           And shall reign with him a thousand years.'

I will close this lecture with a few passages giving the text
in its poetic form in order that its force and beauty may be
better appreciated.   The first is a vision of the future blessedness of those who had been sealed and suffered martyrdom :

9 'After these things I saw
           And behold a great multitude which no man could
                number,   .

vii. 9-10,
13-17. Vision
of the future
blessedness

---

[1] The detection of this interpolation is due to Mr. Marsh.

[2] See p. 35, note, on this rendering.

[3] This couplet is found in the manuscripts at the beginning of ver. 4,
where alike the context and the grammar are against them.

of those who
had been
sealed and
suffered
martyrdom.

Out of every nation and (all) tribes and peoples, and
    tongues,
Standing before the throne and before the Lamb,
Clothed in white robes, and with palms in their hands;

10 And they were crying with a loud voice, saying,
Salvation to our God
That sitteth upon the throne,
And unto the Lamb.

13   And one of the elders answered saying unto me,
These which are clothed in white robes, who are
14 they, and whence came they? And I said unto him,
My Lord, thou knowest, and he said unto me,

These are they that have come out of the great
    tribulation,
And have washed their robes,
And made them white in the blood of the Lamb.

.15 Therefore they are before the throne of God;
And they serve him day and night in his temple:
And he that sitteth upon the throne shall abide upon
    them.

16 They shall hunger no more,
Neither shall they thirst any more,
Neither shall the sun smite them any more nor any
    heat.

17 For the Lamb that is in the midst of the throne
shall be their shepherd,
And shall guide them unto the fountains of the
    waters of life:
And God shall wipe away all tears from their eyes.'

The next passage is the dirge of the merchants over the
destruction of Rome:

xviii. 11–16.
Dirge of the
merchants
over the fall
of Rome.

11 ' And the merchants of the earth shall weep and mourn
over her,
For no man buyeth their merchandise any more—

12 Merchandise of gold and silver, and precious stones
and pearls,
And fine linen and purple, and silk and scarlet,
And all thyine wood, and every vessel of ivory, and
    every vessel of most precious wood,
And brass, and iron, and marble:

13 And cinnamon, and spice, and incense,
And ointment, and frankincense, and wine,
And oil, and fine flour, and wheat,
And beasts, and sheep, and souls of men.

15   The merchants of these things, who were made
      rich by her, shall stand afar off for the fear of her
      torment, weeping and mourning, saying,

16   Woe, woe to the great city,
      That was clothed in fine linen and purple and scarlet,
      And adorned with gold, and precious stone, and pearl;
      For in one hour are so great riches laid waste.'

The last is the dirge of the Seer over Rome, his appeal to
the inhabitants of heaven to rejoice over its doom, and the
response of the heavenly hosts to the Seer's appeal in xviii. 14,
20, 22–24, xix. 1–4, xvi. 5^{bc}–7, xix. 5–9. The dirge consists of
eight stanzas of two lines each, and the Seer's appeal of two
stanzas of three lines each. The response of the heavenly hosts
is more elaborate. First we have a strophe consisting of three
lines and three lines and two lines, sung by two angels, and a
second of exactly the same structure sung by the Elders or
Cherubim. Then in a third strophe, in answer to a voice from
the throne, the whole multitude of God's servants, Cherubim,
Elders, and the martyr host thunder forth with a voice as of many
waters their praise to God and their joy that the morning of the
Lamb has come. This vision closes with his fourth beatitude :

14   'And the fruits which thy soul lusteth after
          Are gone from thee ;

      And all the dainties and the splendours
          Are perished from thee.

22^{abcd} And the voice of the harpers and singers
          ⟨Shall be heard no more in thee⟩ ;[1]

      And ⟨the voice⟩ of the flute players and trumpeters
          Shall be heard no more in thee.

23^{cd} And the voice of the bridegroom and the bride
          Shall be heard no more in thee ;

22^{ef} And no craftsmen of whatever craft
          Shall be found any more in thee :

22^{gh} And the voice of the millstone
          Shall be heard no more in thee :

23^{ab} And the light of the lamp
          Shall shine no more in thee.

20   Rejoice over her, thou heaven,
      And ye saints, and ye apostles, and ye prophets ;
      For God hath given judgement in your cause against
          her.

xviii. 14, 22, 23^{a-d}. Dirge of the Seer over Rome.

Seer's appeal to the hosts of heaven to rejoice over the doom of Rome.

---

[1] See my _Commentary_, vol. ii. 109 sq.

23[f]   For with her sorcery were all the nations deceived.

24   And in her was found the blood of the prophets and saints,
And of all that had been slain upon the earth.'

Following the Seer's appeal comes the response of the heavenly hosts in three strophes, each consisting of three lines + three lines + two lines. The first is sung by the angels, the second by the Elders and Cherubim, and the third by all God's servants, angels, Cherubim, Elders, and the martyr host :

xix. 1   ' After this I heard as it were a great voice of a mighty multitude in heaven, saying,

xix. 1-3. First strophe— Song of the angels.

Hallelujah ;
Salvation, and glory, and power, belong unto our God :

2   For true and righteous are his judgements ;

For he hath judged the great harlot,
That corrupted the earth with her fornication,
And he hath avenged the blood of his servants at her hand.

3   And again they said :
Hallelujah ;
For her smoke goeth up for ever and ever.

4[ab]   And the four and twenty elders and the four living creatures fell down and worshipped God that sitteth on the throne, saying,

xix. 4[c], xvi. 5[bc]-7. Second strophe—Song of the Elders and Cherubim.

4[c]   Amen, Hallelujah ; [1]

xvi. 5[bc] Righteous art thou, which art, and which wast
Holy, in that thou hast thus judged :

6   Because they poured out the blood of saints and prophets,
Thou hast given them blood also to drink : [2]
They are worthy.

[1] It will be observed that the remaining lines of this strophe have been restored from xvi. 5[bc]-7, which are at variance with their context there. See my *Commentary*, vol. ii. 120-123.

[2] This clause has a technical meaning in Jewish Apocalyptic and Jewish prophecy as far back as the Second Isaiah. It means that God would cause internecine war to arise amongst the Antichristian nations, i.e. between Rome and the East. This has already taken place in xvii. 12-13, 17, 16, but not in xvi, into which seven lines of this strophe (xvi. 5[bc]-7) have been transposed either owing to a misconception of John's editor or through accident. See my *Commentary*, vol. ii, p. 123. The idea in xvi. 6 is wholly at variance with the entire context of xvi.

7   And I heard the altar saying,

> Yea, O Lord God Almighty,
> True and righteous are thy judgements.

xix. 5   And a voice came forth from the throne, saying,
Praise our God, all ye his servants,
And ye who fear him, small and great.

6   And I heard as it were the voice of a great multitude,
And as the voice of many waters,
And as the voice of mighty thunders, saying,

> Hallelujah:
> For the Lord God Almighty hath become King.
> Let us be glad and rejoice;
>
> And give unto him the glory:
> For the marriage of the Lamb hath come,
> And his bride hath made herself ready.

xix. 6ᵈ-8.
Third
strophe—
Song of
all the
angelic and
of the martyr
host.

8   Yea, it hath been given unto her to clothe herself
In fine linen bright, pure.

9   And he saith unto me, Blessed are they which are
called to the marriage supper of the Lamb.'

Fourth
Beatitude.

In the passages which I have just quoted from chapters
xviii-xix you cannot fail to have noticed dislocations of the
text. The full grounds for the above reconstructions of
the text cannot be given here. But many of them commend
themselves even on a cursory examination. I will give only
a few of the more obvious grounds for restoring xvi. 5ᵇ-7
to its original context in xix. The symmetrical structure
of the three strophes, each strophe consisting of two stanzas
of three lines each followed by one of two, at once claims
attention. This structure occurs nowhere else in our author.
This fact in itself points probably to their immediate connexion with each other, and especially as the first and third
strophes and one line of the second strophe are found in
chapter xix, and the seven missing lines with the introductory
words xvi. 7ᵃ of the second strophe are found in xvi.
A little closer study of the fragmentary seven lines in
xvi shows that they are wholly out of place in xvi,
being out of harmony with the thought of their immediate context there. Hence we conclude that these seven
lines must be removed from xvi. If, then, as our next
step, we restore these seven lines, i. e. xvi. 5ᵇ-7, after xix. 4
we find that we have recovered the second strophe in its

Some of the
grounds for
restoring
xvi. 5ᵇ-7 to
its original
context in
xix.

E

original form, and have thereby retrieved the missing seven
lines of the song of the Elders and Cherubim. Finally, we
see that these stanzas, thus brought together, deal all three
with one and the same subject, and this is thanksgiving over
the destruction of Rome, which has just been described in
the preceding chapter.

I will call your attention to one more notable dislocation
of the text. Chapter xiv. 8–20 contains two visions of
judgement. The subject of the first vision is the coming
judgement of Rome, and that of the second vision is the
Messianic judgement. Now to our amazement at the conclusion of the first we read in the traditional text :

xiv. 12–13 'Here is the patience of the saints,
      Who keep the commandments of God
      And the faith of Jesus.
      And I heard a voice from heaven saying,
      Write, Blessed are the dead that die in the Lord
        from henceforth :
      Yea, saith the Spirit,
      That they may rest from their labours :
      For their works go with them.'

xiv. 12–13 should be restored to their original context at the close of xiii. 18, i. e. at the close of the second persecution.

Now what conceivable connexion, we may well ask, have
these words with the righteous judgements just inflicted on
Rome and the worshippers of the Beast in the verses which
precede? None whatever. There is no blessedness of any
kind in store for or connected with the subjects of these
judgements. Hence the words are an intrusion here. And
yet both their diction and singular idiom show that they
come from John's hand. Now if we return to chapter xiii,
we can discover without difficulty where these two verses
should be restored. For first of all we recognize that in xiii
there are two persecutions of the faithful, the first persecution
under the direction of the first Beast, and the second
persecution under the direction of the second. At the close
of the first persecution we find the following significant words
enforcing resignation and faithfulness on the servants of
Christ :

xiii. 10 'If any man is for captivity,
      Into captivity he goeth :
      If any man is to be slain with the sword,
      With the sword must he be slain.

      Here is the patience
      And the faith of the saints.'

Now these last words recall the first words of the intruding verses in chapter xiv. There too we find the words:

> ' Here is the patience of the saints,
> Who keep the commandments of God
> And the faith of Jesus.'

And these words are followed by the great beatitude pronounced from heaven, 'Blessed are the dead that die in the Lord'. Such a beatitude comes in here most appositely; for, whereas the first persecution brought either exile or death on the faithful, the second issued in the death of all the faithful, in the martyrdom of the entire Church. It is most fitting, therefore, that the vision of such a universal martyrdom should close with this great beatitude. Hence xiv. 12–13 should be restored at the close of the second persecution, that is, at the close of xiii.

LECTURE III

THOUGH critical questions connected with the manuscripts and versions cannot receive any treatment in the least degree adequate in these lectures, they cannot be wholly passed over.

Greek uncials and cursives of our text. There are seven uncial manuscripts, and about 223 cursives. Of the seven uncials ℵ belongs to the fourth century, A and C to the fifth, 025 and 046 to the eighth, and 051 and 052 to the tenth. The cursives belong to the tenth century onward to the eighteenth. Their values do not always vary directly with their age, as we shall see presently. Twenty-two of these cursives have been photographed, and several of them for the first time for my edition of the text.

The versions. There are many versions. We have five Latin versions, two Syriac, two or three [1] Armenian, one Sahidic, one Bohairic, two Ethiopic, and one Georgian. I have used the Latin, Syriac, Armenian, and Ethiopic versions directly and the Sahidic and Bohairic indirectly through translations, but have no knowledge of the Georgian directly or indirectly. In any case thirteen versions have been collated for the text which I have published with my *Commentary*. There are also four papyri fragments, whose dates extend from the close of the third century to the fifth.

How are the respective values of these authorities to be determined? To determine the respective values of the above authorities is a task which requires for its solution a general knowledge of the main characteristics of each of the chief authorities, their relation to each other, and above all a mastery of the Johannine grammar.

By their readings in the case of test constructions. I will now take four test constructions (occurring in thirty-five passages) and compare the readings of the various authorities in regard to these. In my last lecture I dealt with these passages from the standpoint of their original form as opposed to the corrected form, which they assumed in

---

[1] Arm.[1,2,3] represent three forms of one version: Arm.[4] a distinct and independent version. There is also Arm.[a], which represents a twelfth-century recension of the older Armenian versions.

thè hands of the successive scribes who copied and corrected
the text.

Now in the peculiar idioms preserved in these passages we
shall find our criteria for distinguishing first-class authorities
from second class, and second class from third.

The first idiom, which is absolutely unique, occurs in the First test
opening words of each of the seven Letters to the seven construction.
Churches. I gave some of the grounds for concluding that
the text of ii. 1 was of the following form:

$$\tau\hat{\omega} \ \dot{a}\gamma\gamma\dot{\epsilon}\lambda\omega \ \tau\hat{\omega} \ \dot{\epsilon}\nu \ \text{'}E\phi\dot{\epsilon}\sigma\omega \ \dot{\epsilon}\kappa\kappa\lambda\eta\sigma\dot{\iota}as,^{1}$$

and that the same abnormal Greek recurred in the other six
letters. In the uncials this construction has been preserved
three times by A and once by C. One cursive directly
supports this construction in one of the seven passages, and
two other cursives indirectly support it (together with A) in
two other of the seven passages, but it has been corrected by
the remaining five uncials, and the remaining 220 cursives, into

$$\tau\hat{\omega} \ \dot{a}\gamma\gamma\dot{\epsilon}\lambda\omega \ \tau\hat{\eta}s \ \dot{\epsilon}\nu \ \text{'}E\phi\dot{\epsilon}\sigma\omega \ \dot{\epsilon}\kappa\kappa\lambda\eta\sigma\dot{\iota}as.$$

Thus the uncial ℵ proves that there existed as early as the
fourth century a school of scribes who deliberately corrected
and normalized the text in these seven passages, and, as
we shall see presently, in other passages where other genuine
Johannine solecisms occurred.

Thus from this comparison A emerges as first almost Result of
without a second. applying this test to the

The second place is taken by C and three cursives, while Greek manu-
the remaining five uncials and the 220 cursives must be scripts : A stands almost
relegated to the class of authorities which have not in a single alone in the right ;
instance kept the faith.

Turning from the manuscripts to the versions, we discover and versions.
that one or other of the three Armenian versions attest the Armenian
original text in all seven passages, that the older Syriac versions first ; the
version attests it in four, the Latin version of Primasius, older Syriac
which is practically that of Cyprian, in four (if not in seven and Prima-
as Hort contends), the later Syriac Version in two and the versions
Sahidic in one. But if Hort's contention is right, Primasius' next.
Latin version and the older Syriac support the original text
in all seven passages, and the Vulgate in one. Here, there-

---

[1] See above, p. 39 sq. See my *Commentary*, vol. i, pp. clvi sq., clx sq.;
vol. ii, p. 244.

fore, the versions attest the original text in the three passages where the Greek manuscripts fail us.

Second test construction. Here A's excellence not so obvious, since there was hardly any temptation to scribes to change construction.

The next Greek construction which I will adduce for our present purpose is ὁ καθήμενος ἐπὶ τὸν θρόνον.[1] In my last lecture (p. 38 sq.) I dealt with the idiosyncrasies of our author in regard to this phrase. Now, if we exclude the primitive corruptions in vi. 4, xxi. 5, and also the passages where the editor has intervened and changed datives and accusatives such as ἐπὶ τῷ θρόνῳ and ἐπὶ τὸν θρόνον into genitives as in vii. 15, ix. 17, xiv. 15, 16, xx. 11, we find that A preserves the original text nineteen times out of twenty, and that ℵ 025, 046 severally preserve it seventeen times out of twenty. The difference here is not so great, but it shows the superiority of A to the other three. The reason for the comparatively frequent survival of these Johannine solecisms in the inferior uncials and in the cursives is not far to seek. The scribes were not so strongly tempted to correct John's idiosyncrasies in connexion with this phrase, seeing that two of John's three constructions were possible in classical Greek and the third in late Greek, though no other Greek author ever combined these three as they are in John.[2] Here the versions take no account of the differences within the Greek.

Third test construction. A with three cursives alone right.

In the third test construction, i.e. in xix. 6 ὁ Θεὸς ὁ παντοκράτωρ, A alone of the uncials is right along with three cursives, 1, 2023, 2040. A is supported here by seven versions, some of these being the best. ℵ 025, 046 with almost the entire body of cursives and the remaining versions wrongly insert ἡμῶν.

In the fourth test construction, i.e. in xiii. 10:

Fourth test construction. A alone right.

$$εἴ τις ἐν μαχαίρῃ ἀποκτανθῆναι$$
$$†αὐτὸν† ἐν μαχαίρῃ ἀποκτανθῆναι,$$

A alone is right. εἴ τις .. ἀποκτανθῆναι (='if any man is to be slain') is a Hebraism—the same as in xii. 7. On p. 37 sq. I have dealt with this Hebraism. In xii. 7 to our surprise it has survived, though none of the scribes knew what to make of it,

[1] In the LXX κάθημαι is followed by ἐπί with the genitive. Only in a few cases with the acc. See my *Commentary*, vol. i, pp. cxxxii, clxi sq.

[2] See Kühner's *Ausführliche Griechische Gram.*[3], II. i, pp. 495 sq., 499 sq., 503 sq. The genitive construction is the most classical; the dative construction is classical also but less usual; the accusative can hardly be regarded as classical at all, though it is not uncommon in later Greek. In the later Greek the local *upon* could be rendered by gen., dat., or acc. with little difference of meaning: see Moulton, i, p. 107.

and all the ancient versions as well as the modern have mis-
rendered it. In xiii. 10, however, though it occurs twice in A
within the same verse, it has been corrected out of every other
uncial and out of every cursive. Here the versions, of course,
are helpless as in xii. 7, where the same idiom has already
occurred. Thus A stands alone in xiii. 10 against all other
existing authorities. Here we may be thankful that one
authority at all events escaped the destructive activities of
the copyists and correctors to whom we owe the Greek
manuscripts. How destructive these activities were we can
gather from the writings of Jerome. Jerome writing in the
fourth century in his preface to the Gospels[1] complains that,
when he sought to purge the Latin version from the errors
and corruptions with which it was teeming, he was attacked
with every form of abuse, and branded as a forger and
impious desecrator of things sacred. Notwithstanding,
Jerome insisted that it was his duty to correct the wrong
interpretations of faulty editors, the perverse corrections of
overweening ignoramuses, and the additions and changes of
drowsy copyists. The Greek manuscripts suffered similarly,
he states elsewhere. These represent some of the difficulties
with which scholars have to contend in recovering the original
text of the N. T.

I have given a few of the multitudinous passages in which
A manifestly stands pre-eminent and without a rival in the
first class. C though closely related to A has suffered much
at the hands of correctors and may safely be relegated to the
second class, and the other uncials to the third.

The versions are of great value in determining critical
questions, but only in four readings (iii. 1, 7, 14; viii. 12) are
we obliged to fall back absolutely on the versions owing to
the corruption of the Greek manuscripts.

The following genealogical table of the authorities for the Provisional
text of the Apocalypse will enable the reader to see at a glance genealogical
table of the
the respective values of these authorities so far as they are authorities.
known at present. The uncial manuscripts are A ℵ C, 025, 046:

---

[1] See Jerome, *Praefatio . . in quattuor Evangelia*, Migne, vol. x, p. 526
'me falsarium, me clamans esse sacrilegum'. Jerome rejoins: 'tot enim
sunt exemplaria pene quot codices. Sin autem veritas est quaerenda
de pluribus: cur non . . . ea quae vel a vitiosis interpretibus male
edita, vel a praesumptoribus imperitis emendata perversius, vel a
librariis dormitantibus addita sunt, aut mutata, corrigemus?'

The Archetype of John, completed about A. D. 95.

Edited soon after 95 by an unknown disciple with many dislocations of the text and interpolations.

Correction of text begins in the 2nd cent. and goes on steadily but sporadically towards a normalized form of text.

Most primitive form (A. D. 280–450) of text, in which correction has made some progress.

A somewhat normalized and very corrupt form of text which replaces a whole class of the author's constructions by more normal Greek.

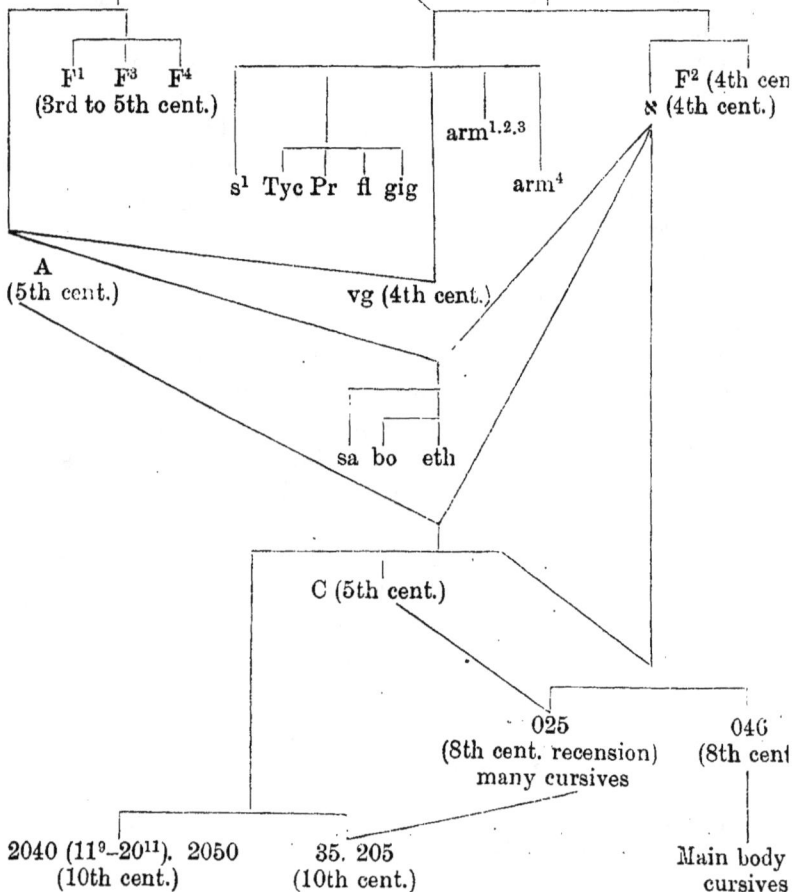

F[1]   F[3]   F[4]
(3rd to 5th cent.)

s[1] Tyc Pr fl gig

arm[1.2.3]

arm[4]

F[2] (4th cen
ℵ (4th cent.)

A
(5th cent.)

vg (4th cent.)

sa bo eth

C (5th cent.)

025
(8th cent. recension)
many cursives

046
(8th cent

2040 (11[9]–20[11]). 2050
(10th cent.)

35. 205
(10th cent.)

Main body
cursives

Four cursives are given—35, 205, 2040, 2050. F¹ F² F³ F⁴
denote papyri fragments. s¹ denotes the oldest Syriac version;
sa the Sahidic; bo the Bohairic; arm^1.2.3.4 the various Armenian
versions; vg the Latin Vulgate; Tyc Pr fl gives older forms of
the Latin version; eth the Ethiopic version.

There are many unities in respect of thought, form, and treatment maintained throughout the Apocalypse. One of the most
important unities of thought,[1] that runs through the entire
Apocalypse, is the belief of the Seer that all the faithful must
suffer martyrdom. This belief appears at the outset in an
indefinite form, but as the action of the divine drama moves
forward, the thought of the Seer becomes less and less shadowy,
till at last it stands forth in such clear outline and is stated
in terms so distinct, that it can no longer be misunderstood.
And not only is this the fact, but owing to this deeply rooted
belief the Seer is compelled to recast the great traditional
expectation of the Messianic Kingdom in accordance with it.

The Seer believes that all the faithful must suffer martyrdom during a world-wide tribulation.

Let me now advance the evidence for the above statements.
The first reference to this expectation appears in the Seer's
words in iii. 10:

First reference to this tribulation (iii. 10) world-wide and affecting only the faithless.

'Because thou hast kept the word of my endurance
I will also keep thee from *the* hour of *tribulation*,
Which is to come upon the whole world,
To tempt them that dwell upon the earth.'[2]

I have italicized the words that are of supreme importance
here. This persecution is to embrace the entire world and to
be distinguished from the local persecutions that have already
occurred, ii. 10, 13: in the next place it is mainly to affect
those that dwell on the earth.[2] As yet there is no reference
to its inexorable demands.

The next note of definition appears in vi. 9–11. In this
vision of the fifth Seal the souls of those who had been
martyred under Nero are seen under the altar in heaven, vi. 9.
These make one definite prayer and only one for retribution

It was to take place within 'a little season' for retribu- tion on the

---

[1] This section dealing with the Seer's belief in a universal martyrdom
did not belong to the original lecture. But the misconceptions of my
critics render its presence here necessary.

[2] For the meaning of 'them that dwell upon the earth, i.e. the
unbelievers, see my *Commentary*, vol. i, p. 289 sq. The demonic tempta-
tions here referred to can only affect the unbelievers. The faithful are
secured in vii. 4–8 against them by the seal of God on their brows.

persecutors
was to take
place when
the roll of
the martyrs
was complete
in the
Domitianic
persecution.
on those that dwell on the earth, vi. 10. They are therefore
bidden to wait 'for a little season' till the roll of the martyrs
is complete, vi. 11,[1] as the Seer expects it will be in the
Domitianic persecution. The implication in this passage is
that when this roll is complete Rome will meet its doom, and
that within 'a little season'. The passage is worth quoting:

vi. 9. 'And when he had opened the fifth seal, I saw under-
neath the altar the souls of them that had been slain for the
word of God, and for the testimony which they held.

10   And they cried with a loud voice, saying,
How long, O Master, holy and true,
Dost thou not judge and avenge our blood
On them that dwell on the earth?

11   And there was given to each one of them a white robe,
And they were bidden to rest yet for a little season,
Until their fellow-servants also and their brethren should
be fulfilled,
That should be killed even as they.'

To enable the
faithful—the
144,000—to
face this
tribulation
they are
sealed with
the seal of
God.
When the judgements of the six Seals have been executed,
there follows the sealing of all the faithful, vii. 4–8. These
are the spiritual Israel, and their number is given symbolically
as 140,000.[2] The object of the sealing is to secure them, not
against death and martyrdom, but against the demonic Woes,[3]
i.e. the great tribulation to which the Seer has already referred
in iii. 10.

That all the
sealed were
to be mar-
tyred is the
implication
of vii. 9–17:
their subse-
quent glorifi-
cation.
When the sealing of the faithful is over, the Seer abandons
the chronological order which he has pursued in iv–vii.8.[4] This
breach in the unity of time is purposeful. The faithful have
indeed been sealed in vii. 4–8, but, since this sealing does not
secure them against physical suffering and martyrdom, the
Seer now recounts another vision in vii. 9–17 in order to
encourage them in the face of these impending evils. In this
proleptic vision the 144,000 who had been sealed and martyred

[1] See my *Commentary*, vol. i, pp. 176 sqq.

[2] On the identity of these 144,000 see op. cit., vol. i, pp. 199–201.

[3] Op. cit., vol. i, pp. 194–9, 205 sq.

[4] Op. cit., vol. i, p. 189. The Seer abandons the chronological order
also in xiv, and with the same object. Hence just as viii follows
chronologically immediately on vii. 4-8, so xv follows immediately
on xiii.

are now seen standing blessed and triumphant before the throne of God.

> vii. 14 'These are they that have come out of the great tribulation,
> And have washed their robes,
> And made them white in the blood of the Lamb.'

After this vision the Seer returns in viii to the chronological order, and represents the silencing of the praises and thanksgivings of the heavenly hosts[1] in order that 'the prayers of *all* the saints', which they offered up in the face of the coming great tribulation, might be presented before the throne of God, viii. 1, 3–5. The implication of course is that the needs of the saints, even of the weakest, are of more concern to God than all the psalmody of heaven. The object of these prayers is that the faithful might be shielded—not from martyrdom—but from the sway of the demonic powers. *Heaven's praises silenced, that the prayers of all the faithful may be presented for Divine help in the great tribulation—the demonic Woes.*

The three demonic Woes now ensue. Their aim is to secure the subjection of all men to the Antichrist. Against the faithful the first two Woes are inoperative; and the third ineffective; for it fails to make the faithful apostatize, though it secures their universal martyrdom, xiii. 15. Here at last the belief of the Seer is stated in the most unmistakable terms. Against the faithless the three Woes are effective. The first two make them more obdurate in their wickedness, ix. 20–21; the third blinds their spiritual vision so that they become worshippers of the Beast and bear his mark on their hand and brow, xiii. 14, 16. *Object of the demonic Woes. The third Woe, though ineffective as regards the faithful, results in their universal martyrdom.*

That the martyrdom should be universal every measure is taken. The definite order is issued that 'as many as should not worship the image of the beast should be killed' (xiii. 15). Thus the sole alternative for the faithful was worship of the Beast or martyrdom. Nay more, all were required to bear the mark of the Beast, xiii. 16. But none could receive this mark unless he first rendered worship. Hence these two indispensable requirements of the Antichrist are conjoined in xiii. 15, xiv. 9, 11, xix. 20, xx. 4. And to secure that none should evade them, the very necessaries of life are to be withheld from all that do not bear his mark, xiii. 17, that is, from all that refused to render him worship. *Every measure taken to make the alternative—worship of the Beast or death—inevitable. Requirements of the Antichrist. Non-compliance entailed economic paralysis and actual death.*

---

[1] Op. cit., vol. i, pp. 218 sq., 221 (*ad fin.*), 223.

We may observe that the great beatitude pronounced ,by God Himself, which by an error of the copyist was transferred into the midst of the punishments of the faithless in xiv, can

Loyalty even unto death of all the faithful acknowledged and crowned by a divine beatitude. only rightly be read at the close of the persecution which was to be enforced by the second Beast and result in the martyrdom of all the saints.[1] There is no other place for it in the Apocalypse, and its supreme fitness at the close of this persecution cannot fail to be manifest to every reader :

xiv. 12 ' Here is the patience of the saints,
Who keep the commandments of God,
And the faith of Jesus.

13   And I heard a voice from heaven saying,.

W.rite, Blessed are the dead which die in the Lord
from henceforth :
Yea, saith the Spirit,
That they may rest from their labours ;
For their works go with them.'

At the close of xiii with its beatitude the Seer again breaks with the chronological order in xiv with the view of encouraging his readers, as in vii. 9–17, to face the dread alternative that awaits every one of them, as he has just

Proleptic vision of the glorified saints on Mt. Zion— the 144,000 who had been sealed in vii. 4–8 and martyred in xiii. shown.   Hence in xiv. 1–5 we have a second proleptic vision, in which the entire body of the faithful, who had undergone martyrdom in xiii, are represented on Mount Zion along with the Lamb—during the Millennial reign.[2] These are the mystical 144,000, xiv. 1, 3. The Seer is careful, by attaching the same mystical number to the group in vii. 4–8, and to that in xiv. 1–5, to make their identity unmistakable.[3] Here again the expectation of the Seer is expressed in sufficiently explicit terms.

At the close of xiv, which is wholly proleptic, the Seer in xv again returns to the chronological order of events.

Further vision of the saints who had been martyred in xiii. Chronologically xv follows immediately on xiii. xv opens with a vision of the entire martyr host that had fallen in xiii but are now in heaven. Characteristically the events of xiii are recalled in xv. 2 in the phrase describing the martyrs

---

[1] See p. 50 sq., and my *Commentary*, vol. i, pp. 368–73.
[2] Op. cit., vol. ii, pp. 4, 422.
[3] On the identity of the 144,000 in vii. 4–8 and xiv. 1–5, see op. cit., vol. i, pp. 199–201, 206, 209 ; vol. ii. p. 5.

as 'those that had been victorious over the beast and over his image'. The roll of the martyrs referred to in vi. 11 is now complete. Hence the triumphant psalmody in heaven and the singing of the new song known only to the 144,000.

We may pass by the judgements of the Seven Bowls, xvi, which affect only the heathen world.

The roll of the martyrs being now complete, the time has come for the judgement of Rome in xvii–xviii. This was not to take place till this roll was complete, as we have already seen in vi. 11.

Once more we are obliged to recognize the effect of the Seer's belief in his description of the Millennial Kingdom. If the world were to be evangelized afresh, as is promised in xi. 15, xiv. 6–7, xv. 4,[1] this evangelization could only be effected through supernatural intervention, seeing that all the faithful were to be martyred before the advent of the kingdom. Hence the Seer recasts the traditional doctrine of the Millennial reign. 'Hence our Seer expected Christ to return on His Second Advent with all the blessed martyrs to destroy the declared enemies of the kingdom (xvii. 14, xix. 11–20) and to found the Millennial Kingdom in the Jerusalem that was to come down from heaven, and so to evangelize the world afresh (xxi. 9–xxii. 2, 14–15, 17, xx. 4–6).'[2]

Thus this expectation of the Seer affects his entire work from the beginning to its close. Among the smaller unities maintained and developed within the Apocalypse we might adduce the following. First the seven Beatitudes, the first of which occurs in the first three verses of the first chapter, and the seventh in the seventh verse of the last chapter.[3] Next the judgement demanded by the souls under the altar in vi. 9 is dealt with in various stages of fulfilment,[4]

[marginal notes:] Seer's belief in a universal martyrdom leads to a transformation of the traditional expectation of the Millennium.

Lesser unities maintained throughout the Apocalypse.

---

[1] See my *Commentary*, vol. ii, pp. 149-50.

[2] Op. cit., vol. ii, pp. 456-7.

[3] There is a certain fitness in the order of the seven. The first (i. 3) declares the blessedness of those who read and keep the prophecy; the second (iii. 3, i. e. xvi. 15) of him who watcheth and keepeth his garments; the third (xiv. 12–13) of those who die in the Lord; the fourth (xix. 9) of those who having so died are invited to the marriage supper of the Lamb; the fifth (xxii. 14) of those who had washed their garments that they might have access to the tree of life in the heavenly city; the sixth (xx. 6) of those who have actually part in the first resurrection; the seventh (xxii. 7) of those who keep the words of this Book.

[4] See my *Commentary*, vol. ii, pp. 123-4.

from the eighth chapter to the nineteenth, namely, in viii. 3–4, ix. 13, xiv. 18, xvi. 7 (xvi. 5^b–7 is restored in my edition after xix. 4). Thirdly, the division of the Book into seven parts: 1. John's call and commission, i. 4–20. 2. The problem of the Book as set forth in the letters to the Seven Churches, ii–iii. 3. Vision of God to whom the world owes its origin, and of Christ to whom it owes its redemption, iv–v. 4. Judgements of the World in the Seals, Woes, and Bowls, vi–xx. 3. 5. The Millennial Kingdom with Jerusalem come down from heaven as its cápital, and the casting of Satan into the lake of fire, xxi. 9–xxii. 2, 14–15, 17, xx. 4–10. 6. The vanishing of the first heaven and earth. Final Judgement of the dead by God Himself. 7. The everlasting kingdom in the new heaven and the new earth and the New Jerusalem, xxi. 5^a, 4^d, 5^b, 1–4^{abc}, xxii. 3–5.

Another of the lesser unities that have escaped notice is the fulfilment in the Millennial Kingdom on earth, in xxi. 9–xxii. 2, 14–15, 17, of the promises made in xi. 15, xiv. 6–7, xv. 4.

All these lesser unities contribute to the great unity of thought and development apparent throughout the Apocalypse. But the most convincing argument for the unity of authorship is the unique grammar and style of the Book. This unity of style is discernible in every part of the Apocalypse save in the sources, which our author has taken over in a Greek form, such as xi. 1–13, xii, xvii, xviii, and even in these the hand of our author is constantly manifest alike in the additions he makes and in the new forms in which he recasts the traditional materials.

The unity of diction between different parts of the Apocalypse could in itself establish unity of authorship, but the recurrence of the same idioms throughout the Apocalypse— of idioms in many cases unique and peculiar to our author's style—presents the most irrefragable proof of this unity of authorship.

Seer has made use of sources.

I cannot enter here into the grounds on which it is necessary to assume the existence of sources in the Apocalypse, and this is the less necessary, since practically every first-class authority on the Apocalypse for the last thirty years makes this assumption. The only matter of moment here is to determine, if time would admit, the extent of the sources which our author laid under contribution. But there is no time for such a task in these lectures. I have done this work elsewhere with sufficient fullness, and must content myself with simply stating my main conclusions.[1] These sources, some Christian and some Jewish, are vii. 1–8, xi. 1–13, xii–xiii, xvii–xviii—in all about five chapters. These, together with earlier visions of his own, our author has re-edited and in the main brought into harmony with their new contexts. But the work of editing has not been thorough, and certain incongruities survive in the incorporated sections, which our author would no doubt have removed if he had lived to revise his work. To mention only one of these, let me draw your attention to xii. 14–16. Here we read: 'And there was given to the woman the two wings of the great eagle that she might fly into the wilderness to her place, where she is nourished for a time and times and half a time, because of the serpent.' This passage was written originally either of the Christian Church before A.D. 70, and referred to the escape of Christians from Jerusalem before it was beleaguered by the Romans in 67 or of the flight of certain Jews to Jabneh before A.D. 70. But such an expectation has no place in our author, since according to his view in A.D. 95 no part of the true Church was to escape persecution, and none to escape martyrdom as we have already seen.

Certain incongruities survive in the sources incorporated by the Seer.

The only subjects that call for consideration now are the date, authorship, and aim of the Book.

The external evidence for the date of the Apocalypse is almost unanimously in favour of the closing years of Domitian —in other words for the year A.D. 95. But there are some ancient authorities, though not the earliest, which assign it variously to the reign of Claudian, Nero, or Trajan. The external evidence for these periods is, however, negligible in the face of the practical unanimity of the evidence for the Domitianic date.

Date of the Apocalypse — A.D. 95.

But when the cursory reader of the Apocalypse turns from the external to the internal evidence he is plunged in hopeless bewilderment. And not only is it the cursory reader that is bewildered but also the serious student, as the history of the interpretation of the Apocalypse clearly shows. Thus this book is assigned in the main to three different periods by three groups of scholars, and each group contains the names of men notable for their learning and judgement. One group

Internal evidence points more or less strongly to three different dates.

[1] See my *Commentary*, vol. i, pp. lxii–v, and the various sections, to which attention is there drawn, throughout the *Commentary*.

assigns it to be the closing years of Nero; the second to the reign of Vespasian, and the third to the last years of Domitian.

Now for these three dates internal evidence is indubitably to be found in the Apocalypse. But when these three groups of scholars just referred to deal with the evidence, all but universally each of the three groups fixes its attention on the evidence supporting the particular date it has accepted, and plays fast and loose with the evidence, which conflicts with this particular date, and which just as clearly postulates a different one. *For the scholars who upheld the absolute unity of the Apocalypse and maintained that every word of the Apocalypse came from John the Seer, no other course was open.* To explain the difficulties that beset the particular date they

had adopted they had perforce to explain them away. But to those who on incontrovertible evidence have been obliged to assume the existence of sources in the text as well as the incorporation by the Seer of earlier visions of his own, the occurrence of passages belonging to an earlier period than that of Domitian ceases to be an enigma. Certain sources and visions, belonging variously to the reigns of Nero and Vespasian and clearly attesting such periods, were re-edited by our author and embodied in his text. In their new contexts these sources have assumed in nearly every respect a new outlook and a new significance. I have been careful to say 'in nearly every respect'; for some of the sources that our author has incorporated contain individual details which cannot be interpreted of the period of Domitian to which the book as a whole belongs. As I have stated earlier in this lecture, such inconsistent details would have certainly been excised, had our author had an opportunity for revising his work.

Let me now summarize the results at which we have arrived. These results have to do with most of the critical questions connected with the Apocalypse. We have seen how by a study of the manuscripts, the versions and papyrus fragments, we have been enabled to classify these authorities and determine their relative values in recovering the original

text. Having recovered this text, so far as these authorities are in themselves adequate for this purpose, we have next studied the diction, idiom, and grammar of our author. This study has enabled us to determine more accurately the respec-

tive values of the manuscripts and versions, and made us
competent to appreciate the absolutely unique style of John
the Seer; to recognize interpolations, especially those inserted
by the hand of John's first editor, and so to eliminate those
elements which are destructive to the sense of their immediate
contexts, and which have stood between John and his readers
from the close of the first century to the present day.

us to recognize the interpolations of John's editor, his dislocations of the text, and his general incompetence as an editor,

In this connexion also we have discovered various dislocations of the text, some of which were due to this editor's
adaptation of the text to his interpolations and others to his
sheer incapacity to understand his master's work.

But the critical study of John's grammar has rendered
still further service. For by its help we have been enabled to
recognize as Hebraisms phrases which hitherto have been
either obscure or wholly unintelligible, and so a flood of
light and meaning has been thrown on the text.

and led to a recognition of the Hebraistic character of the text.

Again, we have seen that the Apocalypse is not a prose
work, such as it is represented in every manuscript and every
great version since the second century. On the other hand, we
find that it is full of poetry from the first chapter to the last,
that its author has adopted various poetical forms as the best
vehicles for the expression of his thought, and that even the
literal translation of his words in these forms bears the
indelible stamp of poetry. We have already learnt that
the recognition of the poetic form of the Apocalypse has
contributed both to the recovery of the text in individual
passages, to the restoration of the right order in dislocated
passages, and to the discovery of our author's thought.

Its poetical character, which has also proved to be of critical value in the recovery of the text.

Once more, we have reviewed the various methods of interpretation which have been used by scholars in their works
on the Apocalypse. Whilst we have found that some are
wholly inapplicable to our author's work, we have recognized
that others are essentially necessary. Of these the chief are
the Contemporary-Historical, the Eschatological, the Literary-
Critical, and the Philological.

We have learnt to discriminate between the various methods of interpretation.

Now before we pass from this subject of the methods of
interpretation it may be well to emphasize one or two truths
in connexion with Old and New Testament prophecy in
general. Though every prophecy was directed to the events of
the author's time, and to future events so far as they arose out
of them, no true prophecy was limited to its immediate
object, but, so far as it was a setting forth of God's mind,

Though prophecy was directed to contemporary events and the

F

future so far as it rose out of them, no true prophecy is limited to its immediate objects, in fact need not be fulfilled in respect of these; yet sooner or later they must be fulfilled in divers manners and degrees of completeness.

it was true for all time and for all like crises in human affairs. Thus, though every great prophecy was directed to the events of the author's own time, it was not necessarily fulfilled at all in regard to its immediate object; and even if it were fulfilled, its truth could not be limited to or be exhausted by any such event or series of events. There is always a human and fallible element in every prophecy. The perspective of the prophet was frequently, or, shall we say, nearly always wrong. He was too impatient with God's methods of governing the world. When he did venture on definite predictions or detailed forecasts, these predictions and forecasts were never literally realized. But all great moral and spiritual truths enunciated by the prophets will and must of a surety be fulfilled at sundry times, and in divers manners, and in varying degrees of completeness. Such truths are timeless and creative, and sooner or later they take shape and find their embodiment in the actual events of history.

The task of the prophet is not prediction but the setting forth of the mind of God.

The essential office of the prophet is not prediction at all. The greatest prophets may never give utterance to a single prediction. The prophet's imperative task is to set forth the mind of God. Hence it is the office of the prophet to bring home to his nation or the world at large the true ideals and destinies of the individual, of the nation and of the world, and if he achieves this end in his interpretation of a national or world crisis, then he is a true prophet, though his forecast of the immediate future may be mistaken. Nay more, such a prophecy is not to be judged by its literal

True function and value of prophecy.

fulfilment in subsequent history, but by its power to arouse the dormant conscience, to emancipate men from the yoke of materialistic motives and ends, to bring them under the sway of spiritual ideals, to quicken their faith, and to wake in them a living consciousness of God and righteousness, of judgement and eternity.

We have now studied the Apocalypse from various aspects. The time is fast drawing to a close, and in what remains it would seem best to limit myself to some account of our author and his object.

Is the name John a pseudonym? All Jewish Apocalypses

Now first of all we may ask, Who was our author? Was his name John, as the Book asserts, or was this name a pseudonym? There are good grounds for this question, seeing that all Jewish apocalypses from the third or second

century B.C. down to the latest work of this literature in from 300 B.C. onwards are pseudo-nymous.
Judaism were all pseudonymous. Seeing then that in Judaism
from the third century B.C. onwards all literature of this
type is pseudonymous, and that the author of the New
Testament Apocalypse was a Jewish Christian, why do we
not at once assume that the Apocalypse is also pseudonymous?
The only Old Testament work which is essentially apocalyptic
in character, and not pseudonymous,[1] is the Book of Joel,
and it is not later than the fourth century B.C.

The reasons which led Jewish writers to issue their writings The grounds for such pseudo-nymity.
pseudonymously I have set forth on several occasions, and
these are as follows: 'From the time of Ezra onwards the
Law made steady progress towards a position of supremacy
in Judaism, and just in proportion as it achieved such
supremacy, every other form of religious activity fell into
the background. This held true even of the priesthood . . .
But in an infinitely higher degree was it true of prophecy.
When once the Law had established an unquestioned
autocracy, the prophets were practically reduced to the
position of being its exponents, and prophecy, assuming a
literary character, might bear its author's name or might
be anonymous. When a book of prophecy brought dis-
closures beyond or in conflict with the letter of the Law, it
could hardly attain to a place in the Canon. This was the
case we know with Ezekiel, which narrowly escaped being
declared apocryphal by Jewish scholars (Shabb. 13ᵇ; Men. 45ᵃ)
as late as the first century of the Christian era.

'The next claim made by the Law was that it was all-
sufficient for time and eternity, alike as an intellectual creed,
a liturgical system, and a practical guide in ethics and
religion. Thus theoretically and practically no room was left
for new light and inspiration, or any fresh and further dis-
closure of God's will: in short, no room for the true prophet—
only for the moralist, the casuist, and the preacher. How,
therefore, from the third century onward, was the man to
act who felt himself charged with a real message of God
to his day and generation? The tyranny of the Law and

---

[1] Isa. xxiv–vii, not to mention very many other late and apocalyptic
sections in the Prophets, is virtually pseudonymous, though not in-
tentionally. By the inclusion of these chapters in Isaiah they came
to be regarded as the work of Isaiah.

the petrified orthodoxies of his time compelled him to resort to pseudonymity.' [1]

It was on such grounds that Daniel and other Jewish writers were obliged to issue their appeals to the nation under the names of ancient worthies, who had lived before or not later than the time of Ezra.

With advent of Christianity the grounds for pseudonymity—at all events for the first century of the Christian era—ceased to exist.

But with the advent of Christianity the grounds for pseudonymity disappeared—disappeared, that is, in the Christian Church which came forth from Judaism. The Law was thrust into a wholly subordinate place. In the Sermon on the Mount different precepts of the Law are introduced by the words, 'It was said to them of old time'; but these are followed by the enunciation of a law that subsumes and transcends them with the words, 'But I say unto you'. Similarly St. Paul (Gal. iii. 24) calls the Law a παιδαγωγός— a tutor that guards us in our childhood till we attain our manhood in Christ. And the same attitude towards the Law is conspicuous in the Apocalypse; for it does not mention the Law once throughout its entire compass.[2] Prophecy has now taken the first place. The heavens had opened and the divine teaching had come to mankind, no longer in books of the O. T. or of later ages, whether authentic or pseudonymous, but on the lips of living men, who came forward as heaven-sent messengers of God to His people.

'Thus the spirit of prophecy descended afresh on the faithful, belief in inspiration awoke anew, and for many generations no exclusive Canon of Christian writings was established. The causes, therefore, which had necessitated the adoption of pseudonymity in Judaism, had no existence in the Christianity of the first century, and accordingly there is not a single *a priori* reason for regarding the N. T. Apocalypse as pseudonymous. . . . In 2 Thess. ii. and 1 Cor. xv we have the Pauline apocalypse given under its author's name, and every kind of evidence tends to prove that the greatest of all the Apocalypses was written by the prophet John, who claims to have been its author.'[3]

[1] From my *Commentary on Daniel*, pp. xv sq.

[2] The *differentia* between Jewish and Christian Apocalypses is just this, that, whereas in the former the Law takes the chief place, in the latter it takes quite a secondary position or is not mentioned at all.

[3] Quoted from my *Religious Development between the Old and New Testaments*, pp. 45 sq.

If it had been pseudonymous its author would have claimed to be the Apostle, or at all events John the Elder, who was well known to the Churches of Asia Minor. But he never calls himself either an apostle or an elder. He simply calls himself 'a prophet', and writes as a spiritual father in God to the Christians of Asia Minor. Again, he does not like the authors of Jewish apocalypses say that his book was written for far-distant ages as they were bound to do, but John writes for his own generation, and the date of the book is known to within six months of its completion.

John then writes as a spiritual teacher well known to the Churches of Asia Minor, but he is not John the Apostle nor John the Elder. Unfortunately we know nothing about him from tradition, save what we may infer from a statement of Papias, that there were two tombs bearing the name of John in Ephesus. Now since Papias wrote about A.D. 130 or earlier, and since no Church writer or historian [1] down to A.D. 180 either mentions or even alludes to any residence of John the Apostle in Ephesus or to any visit paid by him to that city, it follows that, if this statement of Papias is trustworthy, neither of the two Johns here mentioned was the Apostle. Who then were these two Johns whose tombs were held in reverence by the Church of Ephesus? Now besides the Apostle we know of only two other Johns, who can be connected with Ephesus. Of these two Johns the author of the Apocalypse was undoubtedly one—the other was most probably John the Elder, to whom reference is made by Papias, Dionysius of Alexandria, and Eusebius. Recent research tends to show that Papias was a pupil of John the Elder. Now Papias was a bishop in Asia Minor, and had frequent intercourse with the great teachers of sub-apostolic times, among whom John the Elder is expressly mentioned. There are some legends which connect John the Apostle with Ephesus, but these are late, as we have seen above, and may be safely left out of consideration in this short summary.

Since we have no historical reference to John the Seer save the highly probable one just mentioned regarding his tomb in

Side notes: If the Book had been pseudonymous, it would have claimed to be the work of John the Apostle or John the Elder, i. e. some well-known personage.

But the Seer is not the Apostle nor the Elder.

The two Johns connected with Ephesus were John the Seer and John the Elder.

---

[1] Excepting the heretic, Leucius Charinus, who wrote the Acts of John probably between 160–80. To this writer, who taught the existence of two gods—a good and an evil one, we owe also the legend that John the Apostle was cast into a bath of boiling oil and emerged from it none the worse but rather the better.

Ephesus, all that we can learn about him must be derived from his writings.

But what are his writings? Now first of all the Apocalypse and the Gospel proceed from different authors. This conclusion has been arrived at by slow and careful criticism, beginning with Dionysius the Great of Alexandria, and may now be accepted as an established fact.[1] Further disputation on this matter here would be mere waste of time. To the question of the authorship of the Epistles we must turn aside for a few moments, seeing that some distinguished scholars, Bousset, Schmiedel, von Soden, and Moffatt, assert that 2 and 3 John were written by the author of the Apocalypse. But this view cannot be maintained. In fact, it can be proved to demonstration that John the Seer did not write these two Epistles, but that they are derived from the same hand which wrote the Gospel, and this, I believe, I have succeeded in doing in my *Commentary on the Apocalypse*.[2] This investigation drew me away most reluctantly from other studies more nearly allied to my main subject. But, before I had completed the investigation, I became very grateful to these scholars for the hypothesis they put forward on this question, since it led me to examine their thesis exhaustively, and in the course of this examination I came upon what bids fair to be a trustworthy, though partial, solution of the Johannine problem—a problem on which no two scholars have agreed hitherto.

Here I may remark that the researcher never knows where his researches are taking him. Even the most insignificant problem, if honestly and thoroughly studied, may lead him to the solution or a partial solution of the greatest. His experience will frequently be that of Saul when he went forth in quest of his father's asses; for we read that when he was earnestly engaged in this humble quest, he found a kingdom.

Now the solution of the problem of the Johannine authorship to which the above investigation led me may be put shortly as follows. First, a thorough application of his philological method proves that the Gospels and Epistles are from the same hand; and that, whereas the Gospels and

[1] See my *Commentary*, vol. i, pp. xxix–xxxiv.
[2] Vol. i, pp. xxxiv–vii.

Epistles are at one in their leading idioms and in their style as a whole, the Apocalypse differs from them exactly in these respects. Secondly, 2 and 3 John were written, as they claim to be, by 'the Elder' and not by the Apostle. If the writer of 3 John had been the Apostle, he could not have failed to invoke his apostolic authority in dealing with Diotrephes (3 John 9), who was disturbing the peace of the Church. 'The Elder' was a well-known figure in the Church in Asia Minor as we know from Papias. Thirdly, we conclude that the Elder wrote both the Gospel and the Epistles, since the philological evidence proves that they come from one and the same author. Thus none of·the Johannine writings in the N. T. go back to the Apostle John.

These conclusions are confirmed by the tradition of the Apostle's martyrdom before A.D. 70, for which there is evidence in several outlying quarters. That evidence of any sort as to John's early martyrdom has survived at all is astonishing in the extreme, seeing that from A.D. 135 onwards Church writers began wrongly but very naturally to assign the Apocalypse to the Apostle. This false conception led to intolerable confusion and the deletion from the pages of most authorities of the account of the Apostle's early martyrdom. When once the legend of the apostolic authorship of the Apocalypse gained currency, men naturally inferred that the Apostle could not have been martyred before A.D. 70, if he wrote the Apocalypse in A.D. 95.[1]

We have then only the Apocalypse to fall back upon for the materials for John the Seer's biography. But this is in itself a rich source of information, and from it we can gather a number of conclusions more or less well substantiated, several of which we have already arrived at in the course of these lectures.

I will now state these without further preface, and, of course, without the detailed evidence on which they are built.

John the Seer, then, to whom we owe the Apocalypse, was John the Seer a Jewish Christian who had in all probability spent the —his biography, so greater part of his life in Galilee; for Galilee was the home far as it can of the Jewish mystics and seers, as we infer from 1 Enoch be gathered and the Testaments of the Twelve Patriarchs. From Galilee Apocalypse. from the

---

[1] For a full statement of the evidence see my *Commentary*, vol. i, pp. xxix–l.

John migrated to Asia Minor and settled in Ephesus, the chief centre of Greek civilization in that province. This conclusion is drawn not only from his very defective knowledge of Greek, and the unparalleled liberties he takes with its syntax, but also from the fact that to a certain extent he creates a Greek grammar of his own, which I have constructed in the course of my studies,[1] comparing it continually with the very different grammar of the Johannine Gospel and Epistles. John the Seer never mastered the κοινή or Greek of his own day. The language of his adoption was not for him a normalized and rigid medium of utterance: nay rather, it was still for him in a fluid condition, and so he used it freely, remodelling its syntax and launching forth into hitherto unheard-of expressions.

Hence his style is, as we have seen, absolutely unique in the three thousand years during which Greek has existed since the time of Homer. That he has set at defiance the ordinary rules of grammar is unquestionable, but he did not do so deliberately. He had no such intention. His object was to drive home his message with all the powers at his command, and this he does in some of the sublimest passages in all literature. With such an object in view he had no thought of consistently committing breaches of Greek syntax. The explanation of this apparently unbridled licence we have found in the fact that he adopted Greek as a vehicle of thought in his old age, and that, while he wrote in Greek, he thought in Hebrew, and very frequently translated Hebrew idioms literally, and not idiomatically, into Greek.

Further, we learn by studying his text that John had a profound knowledge of the Old Testament, and that his thought clothes itself naturally in its phraseology. When he uses the Old Testament consciously he uses the Hebrew text, and generally translates it first-hand, but not infrequently his renderings are influenced not only by the LXX, but also by a later version, which is now lost in its original form, but which was re-edited by Theodotion 100 years later.[2]

John was clearly connected in some way with the author of the Gospel and Epistles. Either these two Johns belonged

---

[1] See my *Commentary*, vol. i, pp. cxvii-lix.
[2] Op. cit., vol. i, pp. lxvi-lxviii.

to the same religious circle in Ephesus, or more probably the author of the Gospel and Epistles was in some manner a pupil of John the Seer, though master and pupil took very different directions, as is not unusual in such cases.

Furthermore, from a study of his text we can with various degrees of certainty discover the books that constituted the library of the Seer. First among these, of course, come the books of the Old Testament. Naturally he makes most use of the prophetical books. Thus 'he constantly uses Isaiah, Jeremiah, Ezekiel, and Daniel: also, but in a less degree, Zechariah, Joel, Amos, Hosea, and in a very minor degree Zephaniah and Habakkuk. Next to the prophetical books he is most indebted to the Psalms, slightly to Proverbs, and still less to Canticles. He possessed the Pentateuch, and makes occasional use of all its books, particularly of Exodus. It is probable, further, that he and his sources drew upon Joshua, 1 and 2 Samuel, and 2 Kings.'[1]

The library of John the Seer. Books of the O.T. used by him.

Of the books which we designate the Apocrypha, there is, so far as I am aware, no indubitable evidence that he has laid them under tribute even in a single passage. In this respect he adopts the attitude of Palestinian Judaism towards this literature, and this is all the more noteworthy, since Paul, James, and the author of the Hebrews are clearly dependent on Sirach and the Book of Wisdom. But, though the Seer adopts the attitude of the Palestinian Jews to the Apocrypha, the grounds for his adoption of this attitude are not the same as theirs. John passed by the Apocrypha simply because it was almost wholly lacking in the prophetic element, just as he ignores many books of the Old Testament on the same ground. But the fact that our author shows no acquaintance with the Apocrypha does not necessarily prove that he was unacquainted with this later literature, which to some extent had its origin, and certainly had its main circulation amongst Hellenistic Jews.

He did not use the Apocrypha.

Next, just as the lack of the prophetic element in the Apocrypha explains John's neglect of it, so its presence in the Pseudepigrapha explains his recourse to this literature. For into this literature the element of prophecy in a true sense does in some degree enter; into Daniel and certain

He used the Pseudepigrapha.

---

[1] From my *Commentary*, vol. i, p. lxv. The evidence is given in pp. lxviii-lxxxii.

pseudepigraphic fragments in the Old Testament, and into
1 Enoch, and other writings of later times in the Pseudepigrapha proper. Of 1 Enoch, the Testament of Levi, and the
Assumption of Moses our author had copies in his library,
and probably of the Psalms of Solomon. There is also
indirect evidence in the text of his acquaintance with a large
body of this literature.

He used
certain books
of the N.T. Of the books of the New Testament he had copies of
Matthew and Luke, 1 Thessalonians, 1 and 2 Corinthians,
Colossians, Ephesians, and possibly of Galatians, 1 Peter, and
James. There is no evidence to prove that the Seer had any
knowledge of Mark. This confirms the conclusion of Professor
Burkitt, who (*Gospel History and its Transmission*, p. 261)
has rightly inferred that all our manuscripts of Mark ulti-
mately go back to a single mutilated copy which breaks off in
the middle of a sentence in xvi. 8, the remaining verses having
been added by another hand.

Besides these books there is no doubt that he had others,
not only by Jewish but also by heathen writers; for the
Apocalypse shows acquaintance with Babylonian, Greek, and
Egyptian myths. In his closing chapters there is an implicit
polemic against the heathen conception of the city of
the gods.

I will bring my lectures to a close with a short statement
of the object of the Seer and of the bearing of his work on
the present world conflicts, political and ethical.

The object of
the Seer. 'The object of the Seer is to proclaim the coming of God's
kingdom on earth, and to assure the Christian Church of the
final triumph of goodness, not only in the individual and
within the borders of the Church itself, not only throughout
the kingdoms of the world and in their relations one to another,
but also throughout the whole universe. Thus its Gospel was
from the beginning at once individualistic and corporate,
national and international, and cosmic. While the Seven
Churches represent entire Christendom, Rome represents the
power of this world. With its claims to complete obedience
Rome stands in complete antagonism to Christ. Between
these two powers there can be no truce or compromise. The
strife between them must go on inexorably without let or
hindrance, till the kingdom of the world has become the
kingdom of the Lord and of His Christ. This triumph is to
be realized on earth. There is to be no legislation, no govern-

ment, no statecraft, which is not finally to be brought into subjection to the will of Christ. The Apocalypse is thus the Divine Statute Book of International Law, as well as a manual for the guidance of the individual Christian. In this spirit of splendid optimism the Seer confronts the world-wide power of Rome with its blasphemous claims to supremacy over the spirit of man. He is as ready as the most thoroughgoing pessimist to recognize the apparently overwhelming might of the enemy, but he does not, like the pessimist, fold his hands in helpless apathy, or weaken the courage of his brethren by idle jeremiads and tears. Gifted with an insight that the pessimist wholly lacks, he can recognize the full horrors of the evils that are threatening to engulf the world, and yet he never yields to one despairing thought of the ultimate victory of God's cause on earth. He greets each fresh conquest achieved by triumphant wrong with a fresh trumpet call to greater faithfulness, even when that faithfulness is called to make the supreme self-sacrifice. The faithful are to follow whithersoever the Lamb that was slain leads, and for such, whether they live or die, there can be no defeat, and so with song and thanksgiving his visions mark each stage of the world-strife which is carried on ceaselessly and inexorably till, as in 1 Cor. xv. 24–7, every evil power in heaven, on earth, and under the earth is overthrown and destroyed for ever.'[1]

On the Christian individual and on the Christian nation the Apocalypse makes claims that cannot be evaded. However often the powers of darkness may be vanquished in the open field, there remains a still more grievous strife to wage, a warfare from which there can be no discharge either for individuals or states. This, in contradistinction to the rest of the New Testament, is emphatically the teaching of the Apocalypse. John the Seer insists not only that the individual follower of Christ should fashion his principles and conduct by the teaching of Christ, but that all governments should model their policies by the same Christian norm. Thus he teaches that there can be no divergence between the moral laws binding on the individual and those incumbent on the State, or any voluntary society or corporation within the State. None can be exempt from these obligations, and such

[1] Quoted from my *Commentary*, vol. i, pp. ciii–iv.

as exempt themselves, however well-seeming their professions, cannot fail to go over with all their gifts, whether great or mean, to the kingdom of outer darkness. It matters not how many individuals, societies, kingdoms, or races may rebel against such obligations, the warfare against sin and darkness must go on, and go on inexorably, till the kingdom of this world has become the kingdom of God and of His Christ.

NOTE

On p. 99 (§ 85, obs.) Driver (*Tenses*[3]) writes : 'No fact about the Hebrew language is more evident than the *practical equivalence* of ויקרא and קרא . . . ו.' This presupposition, which is right all but universally, underlies his explanation of the passages which he gives on p. 138 (§ 117). But, as has been shown on pp. 32-35 above, this presupposition is inadmissible in some of the passages he quotes in § 117. The above two constructions are not universally identical, as has been shown in the notes on pp. 32-35 above.

INDEX

---

[1] καὶ εἶδον only introduces minor subdivisions of the work, but, as the Seven Bowls are a main division, John would have used here μετὰ ταῦτα εἶδον, which in this writer always introduces a new and important vision. Since the latter phrase does occur in xv. 5, we see that this subject of the Bowls is here mentioned for the first time and not in xv. 1 as in the interpolated text. This point is not mentioned in the Lectures. See my *Commentary*, i. clv-clvi, 106-107.